MILITARY PERSONNEL PSYCHOLOGY

MILITARY PERSONNEL PSYCHOLOGY

Written by

DR. ROSHAN LAL ZINTA
Chairman,
Department of Psychology
Himachal Pradesh University
Summer Hill, Shimla-5
&
GAGGAN JOT KAUR
Research Scholar
in the Same Institution

Neha Publishers & Distributors
4832/24, Prahlad Lane, S-207 Ansari Raod, Daryaganj, New Delhi-110002

Published by
Neha Publishers & Distributors
4832/24, Prahlad Lane, S-207 Ansari Raod, Daryaganj,
New Delhi-110002
Tel.: 011-43570976, 23278261
Email-nehapubdistributors@gmail.com

First Edition : 2023

ISBN : 978-93-80318-39-4

Price : 795/-

Laser Typesetting by : Vinod Bhardwaj

Printed at: Nagri Printers, Delhi

PRINTED IN INDIA

Published by Neha Publishers & Distributors, New Delhi-110002

HIMACHAL PRADESH UNIVERSITY
Summer Hill, Shimla - 171005

Professor Arun Diwaker Nath Bajpai
Vice-Chancellor

FOREWORD

It gives me an immense pleasure to know that a book entitled *"Military Personnel Psychology"* duly written by Dr. Roshan Lal Zinta and Ms. Gaggan Jot Kaur, Department of Psychology, Himachal Pradesh University Shimla, is being published from Neha Publishers & Distributors. I am quite optimistic that this book will serve as an important source of knowledge in the field. It seems that serving Nations through the military is really a great instinct in the personnel in general and a matter of great pride to their respective family in particular. By applying their brain, brawn and full faith in the job, the military personnel very effectively, efficiently and courageously serve their motherland more than their own mother by forgetting environmental hazards, family problem and challenging nature of the job.

It seems that the human being since their inception on the planet aspire for safe heaven, thereof are attached with a strong bond to their mother so as to gratify the physiological and psychological need. This system is quite prevalent in animal, birds, insects and other mammalian species. As the child grow up his attachment bond becomes quite firm with place where he live, the land from where he caters his need and the motherland where he keep his head high and give security, freedom, resources and future prospectus. In the particular place, formation of me and mine bond towards loveable things in general and land in particular turn out to be compact and they wants to preserve for long period of time. Therefore, the person at individual and community level in general and National level in particular establishes their territories and committed to defend the same with great vigor. But the greed of the person sometime exaggerates toward the immovable properties especially of land that becomes the source of clashes within the family, neighbourhood, state and the nations. It is one of the reasons that the soldiers of our country are defending the territories with great courage.

It can be seen that not all the time the soldiers through their commanding instincts comes into the profession but the problem of poverty, unemployment as resulted from population explosion, urbanization, landlessness and resourcelessness forced them to join the profession. However, the selected youths considered themselves as very lucky because they got an opportunity to serve the Nation on the one hand and to promote their deprived family in a multifarious ways through their earned salaries on the other. However, some personnel have to pay its cost by loosing their nearer and dearer one including their own life. In initial stage military command, adhering of strict rule and regulation make them vulnerable.

Tel No. 0177-2831363 (Off.), 0177-2815207 (Res.) Fax : 0177-2830775
E-mail : bajpaipersonal@yahoo.com Website : www.adnbajpai.org

HIMACHAL PRADESH UNIVERSITY
Summer Hill, Shimla - 171005

Professor Arun Diwaker Nath Bajpai
Vice-Chancellor

After rigorous training, the military personnel are depated at particular place that may be on high altitude or plateau in nature wherein they have to face the problems in winter, summer, rainy and autumn seasons. Here they have to perform duty by standing from morning to evening and somewhere in day and night. The heavy workload followed with the discrimination based on religiosity (different perception of Muslim, Sikh, Christian and Hindu officers) as well as colour, caste, income and locality bases and under-estimation of capabilities, creativity and intelligence during the duty generate allostatic that in turn enmesh them in psychopathologies.

Despite this, the family related problems in such low paid salaries makes them psychological vulnerable. Further separation stress of family, followed with fear of wife to leave him without sexual contact and children to loose their career and house to be completed before their time further make them emotional. Limited sanctioned leaves and leave slot over expectation of the family members from the concerned personnel on the one hand and the imposed pressure from the authority on the other enmesh them in double-bind situation. Beside this inadequate artilleries and ammunition and quality of machineries with limited capacities during combat situation at the theatric level poses them serious insecurity and death anxiety that make them quite worrisome. Work overload, day night functioning, standing nature of job, marching forward along with heavy burden on their back, standing alone even in dense forest where there is threat to wild animal further increases their suffering. Limited recreational facilities and excessive sleep deprivation, more physical fatigue make them tiresome. More worrisome is that the military personnel are only allowed to work in the job till they proved to be physically vital. So in very young age they have to leave the job and there is no avenue after retirement that creates disgruntlement among them. Further the poor vision of political leaders due to prematurity, poor education and limited experience including poor policies of the government is another reason that increase their psychological vulnerabilities. So, there are various socio-cultural and on job factors responsible behind their grievance. This book has given various perspectives about the psychological suffering of the military personnel in a more comprehensive way. I hope that this manuscript will definitely cater the need of the readers, academicians and students of psychology across the world.

(A.D. N. Bajpai)

Tel No. 0177-2831363 (Off.), 0177-2815207 (Res.) Fax : 0177-2830775
E-mail : bajpaipersonal@yahoo.com Website : www.adnbajpai.org

PREFACE

It is impracticable not to be flabbergast by India where civilization present itself in such a dizzying and innovative burst of cultures, religions, races, and language diversities, intertwining the people in a thread of unity at family, community and National level. The command of its people under burgeoning Himalayas, touching three large bodies of water, and terrestrial beak is unimaginable, where the safeguard and security to the relationship at any level matters a lot. The attachment bond further is generalized to their motherland that they respect and protect a lot. So, if the importance of motherland at family level matter then why not to the government at National level, who have great responsibility to safeguard the people. So, the most youth have inculcated values by their ancestor to safeguard their country and motherland and their encouragement generally help them in selecting military like profession that in fact is a matter of luck and chance. A military is an organization authorized by its greater society to use lethal force and weapons for defending the people of the country by combating actual or perceived threat. Generally word military depict the characteristics of armed force of the Nation, befitting soldiers, and war, etc. Beside this it has its apolitical agenda so as to promote economic expansion through imperialism, and as a form of internal social control. The word personnel deals with a body of person usually employed in the military or armed force to serve the nation.

For maintaining peace on the planet earth worlds political leaders are trying their best by making their country more strong with nuclear weapon. United States in the process has proved very effective in the process whereas the China and Russia are also showing significant growth whereas the India is at fourth position. Aviation Thermobaric Bomb of Increased Power (ATBIP) and hydrogen bomb is Ivan with USSR Top ten countries of in chronological order in military power are: USA, China, Russia, India, U. K. France, Germany, Brazil, Japan and Turkey. India is on the fourth rank which has 1.3 billion active troop, 570 Billion budget, 1130 combat aircraft, 155 major naval vessels, one air craft career and 13 destroyer. An M4 carbine M-16 Ak-47 type95 rifle is world best with China. Ten best future weapons are TDI KRISS Super V XSMG ; CheyTac Intervention M-200 Long Range Rifle

System; Active Denial System, CBU-97 Sensor Fused Air Deployed Bomb, Corner Shot, Metal Storm Stacked Projectile, Boeing YAL-1 Airborne Laser, Dragon Skin Body Armor, SWORDS Weaponized Robot, and 8 Megajoule Electromagnetic Railgun. The most of the strongest weapon lies with United States. Top ten missiles of the words are Congreve, Patriot, Redey, Tomahawk, Sidewinder, Polaris, Nike Ajex, Titan II, Minuteman, and at number one is V2 missile with United State.

Some of the most enduring images of the classical antiquity portray the power and feats of its military Leaders. For example, the battle of Kadesh in 1274 BC was one of the defining points of Pharaoh Ramesses II's 's reign and is celebrated in bas-relief on his monuments. A thousand years later the first emperor of unified China, Qin Shi Huang, was so determined to impress the gods with his military might that he was buried with an army of terracotta soldiers. The Romans were dedicated to military matters, leaving to posterity many treaties and writings as well as a large number of lavishly carved triumphal arches and victory columns. The first reference of armies is found in the Vedas as well as the epics Ramayana, Mahabharata and other classical Indian those have left indelible impression on archery in particular, and martial arts like Dhanurveda in general. The Indian Armed Forces are the military forces of republic India that consists of Army Navy, Air Force and Indian coastal guard, supported by paramilitary forces (Assam rifles and special frontier force) and various inter-service institutions such as the strategic forces command. The President of India is the supreme commander of the Indian Armed Forces that comes under the Ministry of Defence led by union cabinet minister of defense wherein President the Commander-in-Chief of the Indian Armed Forces.

The Indian maritime history dates back to 5,000 years when the first tidal dock appeared at Lothal near about 2300 during the Indus valley civilization at Mangrol in Gujarat coast. The Rig Veda written written around 1500 BC, credits Varuna with knowledge of the ocean routes ; Plava for the stability to the ship and Matsya yantra was used for navigation in the fourth and fifth century AD. The earliest known reference to an organization devoted to ships in ancient India goes to the Mauryan empire from the 4th century BC where emperor Chandragupta Maurya's 's Prime Minister Kautilya in its Arthshastra talks about waterways under navadhyaksha.The powerful navies included those Maurya, Satavahana, Chola, Vijayanagara, Kalilnga, Mughal and Marathaempires. The Cholas excelled in foreign trade and maritime activity, extending their influence overseas to China and Southeast Asia. The Royal Indian Navy was first established by the British while much of India was under the control of the East India Company. The first Indian to be granted a commission was Sub Lieutenant D. N. Mukherji, who joined the Royal Indian Marine as an engineer officer in 1928. Indian sailors started a rebellion known as the Royal Indian Navy Mutiny in 1946, on board ships and in shore establishments which spread all over India. A total of 78 ships, 20 shore establishments and 20,000 sailors were involved in the rebellion. When India became a republic on 26 January 1950, the navy became known as the Indian Navy, and its vessels as Indian Naval Ships. On 22 April 1958 Vice Admiral R. D. Katari assumed office as the first Indian Chief of the Naval Staff. India fought four major wars with its neighbor Pakistan in 1949, 1965, 1971 and 1999, and with China in 1962.

The Indian armed forces have been engaged in a number of major military operations, including the Indo-Pakistani wars of 1947, 1965, 1977 and 1999; Sino-Indian War, 1987 in Skirmish, Kargil, and Siachen. India honours its armed forces and military personnel annually on Armed Forces Flag Day, 7, December. Since 1962, the IAF has maintained close military relations with Russsia including cooperative development on programs such as the Fifth Generation Fighter Aircraft and Multirole Transport Aircraft and modern missile defense systems and nuclear triad. The Department of Defence Production and Supplies of the Ministry of Defence is responsible for the indigenous production of equipment used by the Indian Armed Forces that comprises of 41 Indian Ordance Factories, eight Defence PSUs namely, HAL, BEL, BEML, BDL, MDL, GSL, GRSE and Midhajn. The Indian Armed Forces are currently the Worlds largest arms importer accounting for more than 9% of global imports with Russia, Israel, and to some extent, and France being the primary foreign suppliers of equipment. The country is expected to spend around US$112 billion between 2010 and 2016 on military equipment.

Dr. Roshan Lal Zinta,
Assoicate Professor and Chairman,
Department of Psychology,
Himachal Pradesh University, Summer Hill,
Shimla-17105 (India).

CONTENTS

CHAPTER 1

INTRODUCTION

Why does our Nation have military services? Why are we spending so much money on nuclear-powered submarines–both the "boomers" the huge submarines that carry ballistic missiles and the attack submarines that are supposed to hunt down and destroy vessels of adversarial nations? Why do we have nuclear aircraft carriers–the floating airfields for supersonic fighter aircraft, and the battle groups that accompany them to oceans across the planet? Why do we have stealth bombers? Why do we have am asking these questions, but I hope that you will quickly see that I have not become a pacifist or a foe of our military seeks response of intellectual (Cutler, 2011).

In fact, the above approach of Cutler seems to be quite candid that the human beings in the contemporary scenarios mull over themselves as perilous and petrified from the ascendancy and mugging of commanding people. Its rationale seems to be their advancing wits and redundant progression of science and technology that on the one hand has provided immense security and on the other has spawn cosmic pressure on human well-beings that perhaps was fewer in the lithic period. Perhaps the human being of primitive age were free from religion, rules, and laws to regulate their social life (Deol, 1963, pp. 257) whose will for preeminence followed with egotism and gluttony to inherit properties for their better survival and emotional happiness increased incessantly, in the contemporary scenarios.

It seems that from the moment of birth every human being wants happiness and does not want to suffer. The fundamental proposition is that the human beings ought to be free from fear of psychological and physical intimidation of any kind. The well-being, therefore, is a complex construct that is concerned with optimal experience and functioning. Current research on well-being has been derived from two general perspectives: the hedonic approach, which focuses on happiness and defines well-being in terms of pleasure attainment and pain avoidance; and the eudemonics approach, focuses on meaning and self-realization and defines well-being in terms of the degree to which a person is fully functioning. Ryan & Deci, 2001). Finally, the global well-being involves present life satisfaction, global self-esteem and self-efficacy. The psychological well-being according to Arroyo and Zigler (1995) ranges from positive to negative aspects of well-being to the global aspect of well-being. The positive well-being involves positive affect pleasure on previous day and positive self-esteem. The negative well-being includes negative affect, trait on previous day, anxiety, depressed mood, probability of minor psychiatric disorder and negative self-esteem. Thus, psychological well being is a subjective term that means different, things to different people, is therefore directly related to the personal security.

Personal security is very close to water, food, and shelter on the continuum of basic human needs. Beside this person consider homeland security (Zimmerman, 2011) above than their own security because protection of motherland is much more than to their own mother. As a result, India had a military system as old as civilization whose evidence can be traced from Vedic and Epics literature. Today people in general and various nations in particular are facing various issues related to security thereby "War on Terror" every time grinds them. The real source of insecurity encompasses unsustainable development. Increasing population and decreasing resources have surmounted pressure on their livelihood. Beside this terrorism, communalism, corruption, nepotism and various others have erupted violence that enmeshes thousands of people every year. The un-employment, natural calamity or environmental disaster issues (Nathan, 2004) are competing political, economic, social, and environmental interests behind such problems. Freedoms of citizens in an ever growing number of nations have been becoming intertwined in such a way that individual security is becoming increasingly linked to the achievement of security at the international level through the reciprocal implementation of policies driven by national priorities.

POLITICS OF HUMAN SECURITY

The human security can encompass welter of ideas that was first used in the 1993 in United Nations Human Development Report. According to the Canadian Department of Foreign Affairs, the human security refers to the "safety for people from both violent and non-violent threats." In its broadest interpretation, this definition touches on the right of individuals to live, work and participates without fear in the social, political, and economic structures that virtually affect their lives and livelihoods. While many sovereign States foster these attributes. In truth the concept of human security stands the Westphalian system on its head in that it decrees that the individual (or the collection of individuals known as the nation) is supreme, and not the institutions of governance.

Human security therefore, is an evolving concept that draws our understanding of the physical environment -the web of life in nature and principle of good governance such as transparency, accountability, human right, civil society participation, and international standard setting and cooperation- that sustain the web of life in human environment. It is a people-centered approach which has gained considerable attention in recent years. Brundtland's report of 1987 on sustainable development states that the notion of national and international security transcendence in military power. Further Human Development Report (1998) also popularized the idea of human security that are threatened by various pollutions of the environment (air, water, and deforestation, and desertification, loss of biodiversity and climate change) in general and the dominance of individual, nation and international bodies in particular.

Protective services refers to those services provided to people who are in danger of being mistreated or neglected , are unable to protect themselves and have no one to assist them (NAAPSA, 2001). Step-by step awareness is growing that each nation's quest for security must move beyond the traditional dependency on military security; rather real security requires a holistic co-operative approach that addresses the inter-related threat to humanity. Further, when prolonged inability of individuals to feel in charge of their destiny creates an atmosphere the violence becomes a remedy that increases the range and depth of fear and insecurity. The failed state loses its monopoly over the instruments of coercion - which in the first instance are tied to the judiciary and organs of public order and ultimately, for many nations, the armed forces. To employ an image which many of us a mere decade ago might have considered an anachronism, what follows when this monopoly is lost is the rise of warlords who vie for control of basic human needs - water, food, shelter, and personal safety – through intimidation of those not part of their entourage. For the warlord, power in the form of physical control over an area become key, and the use of force to sustain that power seems paramount. The Military personnel play vital role for providing security to human and Nation. While providing security they have to face various problems. So, it becomes important to study their life.

MILITARY LIFE STYLE

Generally soldiers are patriot, an intelligent, efficient, courageous and disciplined man who loves their mother-land more than their own mother. They had to go up in the open air, under the sea, through the rivers, deserts, thick jungles and over the snow laden high mountainous regions. Our soldiers carry out their mission in infantry squads and platoons, in tanks, in helicopters, and in tactical operations centers. They walk, drive, fly, jump out of aircraft, and sit at consoles. They operate fire arms with millimeter accuracy, fire large caliber ammunition, fire artillery, and control unmanned ground and aerial systems. They also operate sophisticated communications systems and conduct reconnaissance and surveillance directly and with remote sensors. They conduct full-spectrum operations-deciding to go in "hard or soft" based on the combination of commander's intent, immediate cues from the environmental context, and individual judgment. Sometime they had to go without food and water for days together during active operations. They not only fight against the enemies but also with the sickness and problematic situation of the society with their strenuous conditions with smiling face and cheerful dispositions. The soldiers have conscientious and strong faith believe in their duties.

In nutshell, the soldiers are human being those have normal human desires, sentiments and passions. For them it become extremely difficult when they do not even get the news of the welfare of his near and dear for the long time, brutal force of enemy lay down his life, their wife become widow and children as orphans. There is less leisure in their life and is most obliged for his duty. The soldiers put their life at stake to defend their ideals. They have to work more with meager remuneration. Thus the life of the soldiers is full of thorn those sometime have to leave their family after receiving short notice. The soldier with a rifle in their hand frightens and puts everybody out of his wits. Sometime is completely engrossed in killing without any qualm of conscience and haunts the mind of Soldier specially train their sons, infuse in them the glamour of the military profession and prepare them for self-sacrifice for the sake of the country. Generally soldiers have two things in their mind. First they want to push back the aggressor and secondly they wants to vindicate the honor of their family as a soldierly family that spirit also transform in their sons spirit. The soldier's fights for ruling group and become conservative. They help the countrymen in giving peace, love and co-existence. The communism, capitalism and democracy could not live side by side.

It has always remains a great question that what help a soldier most- brain, brawn or faith. Perhaps a better solder must have the entire component so as to make their life as more effective. A soldier should handle very complicated apparatus, wireless set, different kinds of engine, signals, as well as online information, physics, hydrostatics, statistics, and dynamics etc. Resourcefulness should be the greatest qualification for the soldier. Sound mind and sound body followed with better faith can definitely overcome their fear and helps them in victory. A soldier therefore requires common sense, tact, wisdom, fore-thought, initiative and knowledge of life and its affairs. Beside this a good soldiers must possess the quality of leadership to organize things, guide and lead this country. Their cool headedness, equanimity of mind, patience, tranquility and mental poise are of the fundamental importance. They should gain knowledge of geography of area, its terrain, climate and agricultural. Beside this the army should be medically fit because Napolean's army was 50% medically unfit that remains the major cause of his defeat (Deol, 1963).

Army is the leader in human-systems modeling, simulation, and analysis, ensuring that the soldier is considered early in system concept of development. Logistic is the lifeblood of any army that requires quantum leap in strategic responsiveness. Changing how we fight influence changing how we support. The transformation objective is to field a force that is strategically responsive and dominant every point on spectrum of operation. We must build forces based on revolutionary advances in the technology of war that will allow us to keep the peace by redefining war on our term -a future force that is defined less by size and more by mobility and swiftness. That force will be easier to deploy and sustain and will rely heavily on stealthy, precision weaponry and information technology. The transformation challenges the army to balance near term readiness and post modernization in an environment of increased mission and fewer resources. The logistic pipeline must be shrunk, the load lightened and the closing time cut. At the joint level change started with joint vision.

Beside unlimited resources, the army has superfluity of senior and middle ranking officers, combined with a great overall deficiency, mostly in the rank of junior officers. The best and brightest tend to resign and the quality of applicants fails to meet military's need with crime, embezzlement and corruption being rampant especially amongst senior officers. The development of militaries capacities depends on material circumstances (economic), on human resources, and weapons, which, in turn depend on quality and size of a nations populations and its technology. The army has not been spared the changes in mentality. In every spring, military enlistment registration officers are chasing young men who are avoiding their sacred duty. Sometime there is severe hazing, intolerable treatment, and abysmal living conditions reported abuses of commanding officers, including savage beating, torture, extortion, lurid threat and routine humiliation.

The worst of conscription reality is Dedovshchina, which is combined with poor diet and hygienic conditions and lack of effective medical care in the overcrowding barrack. The Dedovshchina start with routine demands for young conscripts to clean toilets, wash older soldier's socks. The defiant are beaten, raped tortured and killed. Thereby shooting and suicidal tendencies are very high. On the one hand government expects too much from them and on the other their own families expect too much from them. As long as our country has a military, our soldiers should be prepared to face the hazards and horrors they may experience. The army thus has to face problems of an extreme complexity. It may includes its loss of its political foundations, material and structural problems, national conflicts and multiplicity hot spots, a general denial of the military services. Therefore, it becomes necessary to epitomize their traumas.

EPITOMIZING MILITARY TRAUMAS

Military service is highly stressful and psychological challenges and difficulties understandably arise frequently. These issues are created or exacerbated by a wide range of features characteristic of military life, such as separation from family, frequent relocations and, especially, deployment to combat zones with ongoing threats of injury and death and exposure to acts of unspeakable violence. The stress of repeated tours of duty, including witnessing the loss of lives of comrades and civilians, can produce extensive emotional and behavioral consequences that persist long after soldiers return home. Serving in today's military often includes dangerous duty (Hoge, Castro, Messer, McGurk, Cotting, & Koffman, 2005; Tanielian, Jaycox, Schell, Marshall, Burnam, Eibner, 2008) that includes lengthy period of separation, frequent geographic re-location and the possibility of death and dismemberment of military member (Cozza, Chun, & Pollo, 2005).

The military personnel faces unique kinds of stressors those are associated with the culture of military as well as agony of combat experience in the midst of an active war zone. The characteristics of combat injuries differ from those of injury normally encountered in civilian practice in terms of epidemiology, mechanism of wounding, patho-physiologic trajectory after injury, and outcome (Champion, Bellami, Roberts, & Leppaneimi, 2003). The nature of combat injury is likely to change because of the changes in the ways war will be fought: recent conflict have been short, high intensity battle in urban or remote area. PTSD symptoms includes painful and intrusive memory, persons avoidance of people, place and things, numbness of feeling, alienation from people, family, friends and associates, developing symptoms of irritability, impatience, anxiety, and depression, becoming rageful and provocative. Sleep problem, hyper vigilance, distrust, attention and concentration problems physical manifestation like heart palpitation and sweating etc (Anderson, 1987).

Any type of war is horrific and devastating for everyone involved. Although ranges of protective factors such as e.g. family and social support mediate the harmful effect of combat stress yet many soldiers and families suffer from acute stress response and health problems. Thus the combat experience is directly related to PTSD, depression and other anxiety disorder (Hoge, Terhakopian, Castro, Messer, & Engel, 2007). Combat stressor may dismantle trust. Deployment stress may affect security of attachment for soldiers. The experience of war deployment has led to the development of symptoms associated with emotional trauma in some service members especially to those who experienced heavy combat. For example 15% or more of soldiers deployed to Iraq in 2007 had acute stress symptoms, 7% had depressive symptoms and another 7% experienced anxiety symptoms (Mental Health Advisory Team, 2008). Members engaged in active combat in Afghanistan and Iraq has experienced traumatic brain injury at rates up to 30% (Tanielian et al., 2008).

Increased risk of deployment exacerbates the stress already experienced by military families (Compas, Connonr-Smith, Saltzman, Thompsen, & Wadsworth, 2000). Aspect of deployment experience such as working with equipment, doing a job, engaging in combat, helping local people, comradeship, quality of leadership, separation from family and quality of food differ from personnel socio-demographic, deployment and military factors (Browne, Hull, Horn......). Although these stressors may negatively impact military youth's ability to adapt to new situation yet some military youths adapt better (Marchant & Medway, 1987). Social connectedness helps in adapting to the family stressors (Barber & Schuluterman, 2008). Psychological state of belongingness occurs when other cares for them (Whitlock, 2006). They become a part of social network (Beam et al, 2002).

Despite this, the military members are regularly exposed to traumatic events that can have lasting effect on themselves as well as to their families (Herzog & Everson, 2010). Although combat exposures have been linked with adverse health outcome yet it is also associated with perceived positive effects such as personal growth and increased resilience (Elder & Clipp, 1989; Schok, Kleber, Elands, & Weerts, 2008). Jones, Murphy, Fear, Greenberg, French, Rona, Wessely, & Hotopf,, 2007). PTSD have different pattern of rewarding and unrewarding perception of deployment

(Ahronson & Cameron, 2007). Generally the conflict of medium term and long term has its consequences on mental health that arouse psychopathological symptoms (Wang, Salihu, Rushiti, Bala & Modwig, 2010).

Research on impact of military trauma suggests that positive and negative from stressful events are separate construct that are largely independent from each other (Britt, Adler, & Bartone, 2007). Research on it indicates that part of part of association between traumatic experience and PTSD is mediated through appraisal (Fontana & Rosenheck, 1998). The most frequent diagnosis was post-traumatic stress disorder. Other diagnoses included anxiety disorder, depression, substance use disorder, or other behavioral or psychosocial problem. Psychological benefit may follow from experience of stressful events but are not limited to coping skills, increased self-confidence, improved military qualification, monetary gain and increased personal experience.

These phenomenon's have been positively labeled as maturity, adversarial growth, post-traumatic growth and thriving (Linely & Joseph, 2004). Research into how individual perceive their deployment experience is an important mean of understanding the association between stressful events and subsequent positive and negative effect (Schok et al, 2008). Research on peacekeeping soldiers has shown that differences that differences in their perception of peacekeeping mission, in terms of how meaningful it was to them were associated with positive effects (Newby et al 2005). After injuries in the war the military personnel has to undergo with various psychological trauma such as incontinence and impotence social difficulties or social assets problems. For example the literature on sexuality after injury has its impact on sexual functioning and reproductive functioning sexual behaviour and adjustment thereof their health (Hugh & de Girolambo, 2007). Traumatic brain injuries can be caused by the bullet or shrapnel hitting the head or neck. It may cause dizziness, sleep problem, memory loss Alzheimer's and Parkinson disease. About 50% of soldier suffers from psychological problems. Family problem can continue after long deployment. Shouting, pushing and shoving are common problems in soldiers. Substance abuse, drug consumption, homelessness, and suicidal or depression problems are common. For example, 1.7 million people served in Iraq about its half suffered from psychological problems (RAND, 2008).

According to De Jong, der Kam, Ford, Hargreaves, van Oosten, Cunningham, Boots, Andrault, and Kleiber (2007) conflict in Chechnya had resulted over a decade of violence, human right abuses, criminality and poverty and a steady flow of displaced refugees throughout the region. At the beginning of 2004 displaced population of Chechnya and Ingushetia were explored. The conflict related factors contributed to ill health Chechnya people (66.8%) felt more unsafe compared to Ingushetia (37.5%) who received more maltreatment, violence and health related problem. Female in military experience more traumas (5.6%) compared to men (5%). Further, 78% female and of 38% of men most probably experience sexual harassment while doing military job. 33% personnel experience physical sexual harassment, 7% as sexual assault and 66% further bar verbal sexual harassment (Wolf, Brown, Kelley, 1993).

Further 46% female in military job have to bear rape; 27% are molested and 49% are physically abused (American Psychiatric Association, 1994). Accumulated evidence suggests an excessive of psychiatric symptoms among veteran deployed 19 the 1991 veteran Gulf War relative to Veteran (Presidential Advisory Committee on Gulf War Veteran Illness, 1996; Iowa Persian Gulf Study Group, in 1997; Fukuda et al. 1998; Unwinn et al. 1999, Kang et al, 2000, Cherry et al, 2001, Hallman et al, 2003). Reintegration of combat service members back into their family is often quite stressful (Doyle & Peterson, 2005) and is frequently complicated by member's trauma and traumatic brain injury symptoms.

Family members of individual exposed to traumatic events are vulnerable to secondary impact of that stress (Figley, 1983). Having a parents with PTSD negatively not only impact adult but also of children (Dirkzwager, Bramensen, Adler, & van der Ploeg, 2005) and marital adjustment (Dekel, Solomon, & Bleich, 2005; Solomon, Waysman, Levy, Fried, Mikulincer, & Benbenishty, 1992)). High level of intrusive thoughts and avoidance symptoms in members with PTSD has been associated with lower level of cohesion, expressiveness, and marital satisfaction (Hendrix et al, 1995). Increasing numbers of mentally ill offenders without concomitant increases in mental health staffing, issues of service utilization and priority populations have become paramount. Shay (2001) captured the horror of psychological injury inflicted by war on the soul and character of soul. Professional must think about combat related mental health issues as psychological injuries rather than disorders. The warriors generally have exposure to combat wherein entire family becomes disrupted with attachment injuries (Basham, 2008). Beside this military operation also exert its impact on environment and health.

MILITARY'S IMPACT ON ENVIRONMENT AND HEALTH

The military intervention across the countries exerts unlimited hazardous effect on the human being. Worlds' military forces are responsible for releasing more than 2/3rd of chlorofluorocarbon (CFC) -113 into the ozone layer. During the Cold War, US Soviet Armed forces produced enormous amount of hazardous waste. As a result of naval accident there were at least 50 nuclear warheads and 111 nuclear reactor littering on the ocean floor, sea and land. The Pentagon generates five times more toxin than the five major US chemical companies.

The US Military is single largest source of pollution. Immediate and long term impact of armed conflict are radiation from nuclear weapon (e.g. Hiroshima and Nagasaki), agricultural degradation, unexpected remnants, scorched earth tactics, massive damage of ecology, destruction of vegetation and oil, spreading dangerous substances, threat to animal, fungi and infection agent, premature birth, birth defect, death, impact on delivery, resource diversion, threat to local industries aviation, transport, electronic and computing. Dynamic process that evolve when he mutually form relationship with environment and depend on it. A better scientific understanding of environment and public pressure of higher standard of governance and stewardship, have led to some important successes in reducing the man-made impact on air, water and land that are endangered human security . But the stresses that the military places on environment have not been receiving the same level of attention. The upcoming World Summit on Sustainable Development at Johannesburg opened up an opportunity to bring the military dimension into the ongoing dialogue of development, the environment and human security.

We must set up a cooperative relationship with the earth, not one of dominance, for it is ultimately the gift of life that we pass on to our children and the generation to follow (Bertell, 2001). The Commission on Sustainable Development (CSSD) and Earth Summit also did some significant step for environment protection. World Summit on Sustainable Development talks about peace security and stability necessary for development. In this connection Stockholm Conference to focus internationals attention on environmental issues was held in 1972 that highlighted the issues related to trans-boundary pollutions. Brundtlands report of 1987 is devoted to place, security, development and environment. It states that international security must transcend the traditional emphasis on military power and armed competition.

UN Conference on Environment and Development (UNCED) at Rio, 1992 known as Earth Summit also reflect the Brundtlands report, considered Warfare as inherently destructive for sustainable development. Peace, development and environment protection are independent and indivisible. The World Commission on Environment and Development combined the concept of sustainable development. Environment stress is also a cause and effect of political tension and military conflict. Nations have often fought to assert or resist control over raw material, energy supplies, and land etc. Vast resources are diverted into arm production, and small amount are spent on the military, that in fact produce pollution.

A better scientific understanding of environment. A militaries activities takes lots of stress on the environment As the campaign to ban landmine and decision of International court of justice on nuclear weapon have , society not only can, but must take responsibility for decision that have traditionally been left to military. More appropriately, the military activities affect the physical environment through pollution of air, land, and water. To adequately deal with state failure, military interveners must be prepared to deal with the reasons states fail initially. These include economic disparity, political corruption, and the proliferation of weapons. Planning for military intervention has to include programs that can sufficiently stabilize conditions of daily existence that will permit non-military organizations to undertake the reconstruction of the civil society that has been destroyed. Police, the judiciary, other official government institutions, as well as political parties and specialized interest groups are essential to the creation of an environment of sustainable human security (Smith, & Stohl, 2000). Because intervention in intrastate conflicts is predicated in the first instance on the breakdown of human security, military forces must institute measures that will facilitate the early restoration of individual security.

So, mental health strain is one of the important factors that is frequently observed among the soldiers. Its example is veterans of three or more deployments, with a third of those showing signs of psychological problems defined as either stress, depression or anxiety (Zoroya, 2011). Studies done years after the Vietnam and Persian Gulf wars showed the rate of post-traumatic stress disorder at the time was 15 percent for Vietnam veterans and 2 percent to 10 percent for Gulf War veterans, the researchers reported. Symptoms of major depression, anxiety or post-traumatic stress disorder were reported by 16 percent to 17 percent of those who served in Iraq, 11 percent of those who were in Afghanistan and 9 percent questioned before they left. The differences were greatest for post-traumatic stress disorder with about twice as many with PTSD after Iraq (12 percent) than Afghanistan (6 percent). Before deployment, the rate was 5 percent, about the same as the general U.S. population.

The troops in Iraq saw more combat, including firefights and attacks, than those in Afghanistan. The Iraq units took part in the early fighting of the war. According to Raddatz (2010) the soldiers took medications for stress in United States Military for trying to band aid major psychological problems through drugs. Provision of alcohol in the military may be one of the reasons for getting rid of psychological problems. The NATO doctrine states that: 'Should the situation be such that humanitarian operations requires wide spread protection and human rights abuses (James, 2010). The balancing of the war-winning and human security goals of limiting wars is too important to leave to either the politicians or to the military, particularly as the numbers of civilian leaders with wartime experience declines.

In 2010 more than 1,34,000 people made call to National Suicide Prevention Lifeline dramatic increase in 18-29 year of suicide in America. An experimental, Army mental-health, fitness initiative designed by the same psychologist whose work heavily influenced the psychological aspects of the Bush administration's torture program is under fire by civil rights groups and hundreds of active-duty soldiers. CSF is comprised of the Soldier Fitness Tracker and Global Assessment Tool, which measures soldiers' "resilience" in five core areas: emotional, physical, family, social and spiritual (Leopold, 2011). Its reason is that tomorrow's war will be a war of minds (Mandal, 2009). Developed in conjunction with several of psychology's top stars, the initiative seeks to assess and enhance soldiers' ability to cope with all of life's challenges, including the mental rigors of combat.

But, the military youths have to face periodic separation from parents, wife and children therefore themselves in general and their families in particular suffer from more behavioural problem (La Grone, 1978) than to civilian families. Military life also has impact on the adolescent life. It directly affects the performance of their children. There is also military re-location stress on their family (Hiew, 1992) that may be buffered by social support (Chartrand & Siegel, 2007). Small challenges faced by military youths such as frequent residential moves and school transition may actually bolster their ability to adapt to other stressors such as parental deployment. Fiedler, Ozakinci, Hallman, Wartenberg, Brewer, Barrett, and Kiepen (2006) found military deployment to the gulf war as a risk factor for psychiatric illness among us troop. Repeated deployments of soldier may toll their life and exert enormous pressure on their families. For this the psychological programmes can boost resilience, increase post-traumatic growth and reduce PTSD in the army.

All above factors exert influence on psychological well-being that ranges from positive and negative aspects of well-being to the global aspect of well-being. The positive well-being involves positive affect pleasure on previous day and positive self-esteem. The negative well-being includes negative affect, trait on previous day, anxiety, depressed mood, probability of minor psychiatric disorder and negative self-esteem. The military life is full of stress that exerts influence on their wellness. The married people experience more distress compared to unmarried counterpart as well as the soldiers belongs to far flung places also experience more traumatic events. The military personnel have to follow the norm of the military that is highly stressful. On the one hand the national security is their top priority on the other hand they are also the common men who have their own family, spouse, children, friends and neighbourhood. The deployment cycle further aggravate their suffering. Nomadic nature of military life makes them prone to psychological and physical stressor. For example the military personnel of rural and hilly areas are unable to bear the heat. Similarly the personnel belonging to plain areas are unable to bear the wave of the cold. Therefore, it becomes necessary to study their wellbeing that involves positive and negative indicators. Therefore, the detailed objectives are as follows:-

OBJECTIVES OF THE PRESENT STUDY

1. *To identify the difference between military personnel and civilian on various dimension of psychological wellbeing (Life satisfaction, wellbeing, self-esteem, depression, alcohol, smoking and substance uses).*
2. *To identify the difference between married and un-married military personnel and civilian on various dimension of psychological wellbeing (Life satisfaction, wellbeing, self-esteem, depression, alcohol, smoking and substance uses).*
3. *To identify the difference between Himachali and Non-Himachali married and unmarried military personnel and civilian on various dimension of psychological wellbeing (Life satisfaction, wellbeing, self-esteem, depression, alcohol, smoking and substance uses).*

CHAPTER 2

CONCEPTUAL FRAMEWORK

To hold the victorious trophies of our revolution, to keep the dirty swine's lips from intruding through the fence of our beautiful garden, we expect all you revolutionary young workers to respond to the call of your fatherland (Gittings, 1969, p. 74)

The basic responsibility of the Army is to safeguard the territorial integrity of the nation against external aggression. Due to the country's long borders encompassing different geographical and climatic conditions such as desert terrain on the west, snow-covered mountains in the north and thick rain fed mountainous jungles in the east, the Army has to constantly prepare itself for diverse challenges. In addition, the Army is often required to organizing relief operations. During natural calamities like flood, earthquakes and cyclones and in maintenance intense counter insurgency operations in Jammu and Kashmir and the north east parts of the country. To achieve these objectives, the Army has to be constantly modernized, suitably structured, equipped and trained for conquer their enemy. During the operation they are socially connected that in somehow on the one hand help them in overcoming negative thought and on the other also exert pressure on them.

CONCEPT OF SOCIAL CONNECTEDNESS

The social connectedness is a psychological term that is used to describe the quality and number of connections we have with other people in our social circle such as in family, friends and acquaintances. These connections can be both in real life, as well as online. The more socially connected a person is in his life, the greater sense of self-control and self-determination he feels whereas the zero acquaintance refers to the observation and judgment of someone with whom one has never interacted. There are six components that have been shown to help a person determine the quality of his interactions and social connectedness with others. These are duration of relationship; frequency of interaction with the other person; knowledge of the other person's goals; physical intimacy or closeness with the other person; self disclosure to the other person and social network familiarity.

The duration is a characteristic of bond i.e. how long the bonding in relationship exists. The frequency of interaction with other persons refers to the total number of social interactions per unit time. Self-knowledge is a term used to describe the information that an individual draws upon when finding an answer to the question "What am I like? And what goal I have to accomplish? An intimate relationship is a particularly close interpersonal relationship that involves physical and/or emotional in nature. Physical intimacy is characterized by romantic or passionate love and attachment or sexual activity. Self-disclosure is seen as a useful strategy for sharing information with others. By sharing information, we become more intimate with other people and our interpersonal relationship is strengthened. It is not simply providing information to another person instead as sharing information with others that they would not normally know or discover. It involves risk and vulnerability on the part of the person sharing the information. The social network familiarity that deals with how familiar the other person will be with the rest of your social circle. The higher a person scores on these components, the greater the quality of his social connectedness.

An interpersonal relationship is an association between two or more people that may range from fleeting to enduring.

This association may be based on limerence, love, solidarity, regular business interactions, or some other type of social commitment. It is formed in the context of social, cultural and other influences. The context can vary from family or kinship relations, friendship, marriage, relations with associates, work, clubs, neighborhood, and places of worship. They may be regulated by law, custom, or mutual agreement, and are the basis of social groups and society and society as a whole.

A relationship is normally viewed as a connection between two individuals, such as a romantic or intimate relationship or a parent child relationship. Individuals can also have relationships with groups of people, such as the relation between a pastor and his congregation, an uncle and a family, or a mayor and a town. Finally, groups or even nations may have relations with each other, though this is a much broader domain than that covered under the topic of interpersonal relationships. See such articles as international relations for more information on associations between groups. Most scholarly work on relationships focuses on the small subset of interpersonal relationships involving romantic partners in pairs or dyads. Interpersonal relationships usually involve some level of interdependence. People in a relationship tend to influence each other, share their thoughts and feelings, and engage in activities together. Because of this interdependence, most things that change or impact one member of the relationship will have some level of impact on the other member.

It is a dynamic system that changes continuously during their existence. Like living organisms, relationships have a beginning, a lifespan, and an end. They tend to grow and improve gradually, as people get to know each other and become closer emotionally, or they gradually deteriorate as people drift apart, move on with their lives and form new relationships with others. George Levinger (1983) model was formulated to describe heterosexual, adult romantic relationships, but it has been applied to other kinds of interpersonal relations as well.

According to the model, the natural development of a relationship follows five stages named Acquaintance (Becoming acquainted depends on previous relationships, physical proximity, first impressions, and a variety of other factors). Buildup (people begin to trust and care about each other); Continuation (mutual commitment to a long-term friendship, romantic relationship, or marriage); Deterioration (signs of trouble, boredom, resentment, and dissatisfaction may occur); and Termination (end of the relationship, either by death or separation). The friendship may involve some degree of transitivity. In other words, a person may become a friend of an existing friend's friend. Such social connectedness is prevalent among a soldier that is hampered during deployment to far flange places. Therefore, generate stress.

NOTION OF DEPLOYMENT STRESS

The stress is a term in psychology and biology, borrowed from physics and engineering and first used in the biological context in the 1930s by the endocrinologist Hans Selye in the that in recent decades has become commonly used in popular parlance. It refers to the consequence of the failure of an organism - human or other animal - to respond adequately to mental, emotional, or physical demands, whether actual or imagined (Selye, 1956). When the person perceives a threat, his nervous system responds by releasing a flood of stress hormones, including adrenaline and cortisol that arouse the body for emergency action. Later broadened and that involves physiological response to any demand.

The signs of stress may be cognitive, emotional, physical, and behavioral. The cognitive symptoms may include memory problems, inability to concentrate, poor judgment, seeing only the negative, anxious or racing thoughts, constant and worrying, the emotional symptoms includes moodiness, irritability or short temper, agitation, inability to relax, feeling overwhelmed, sense of loneliness and isolation and depression or general unhappiness. The physical symptoms may include aches and pains, diarrhea or constipation, nausea, dizziness, chest pain, rapid heartbeat, loss of sex drive, and frequent colds. The behavioral symptoms includes eating more or less, sleeping too much or too little, isolating yourself from others, procrastinating or neglecting responsibilities, using alcohol, cigarettes, or drugs to relax and nervous habits (e.g. nail biting, pacing).

Selye researched the effects of stress and identified three stages. First is Alarm (threat or stressor is identified or realized, fight-or-flight response are made). Second stage is Resistance where an attempt is made to cope with the stress.

Third stage is Exhaustion where body's resources are eventually depleted and person may entrap in various illnesses. Selye published in 1975 a model dividing stress into eustress (enhances functioning) and distress (persistent stress that is not resolved through coping or adaptation, deemed distress, may lead to anxiety or withdrawal). Lazarus argued that cognitive processes of appraisal are central in determining whether a situation is potentially threatening, constitutes a harm/loss or a challenge, or is benign. In response to a stressor, neurons with cell bodies in the Para ventricular nuclei (PVN) of the hypothalamus secrete corticotrophin-releasing hormone (CRH) and arginine-vasopressin (AVP) into the hypophysial portal system. The locus cerulean and other noradrenergic cell groups of the adrenal medulla and pons, collectively known as the LC/ NE system, also become active and use brain epinephrine to execute autonomic and neuroendocrine responses, serving as a global alarm system. The autonomic nervous system provides the rapid response to stress commonly known as the fight-or-flight response, engaging the sympathetic nervous system and withdrawing the parasympathetic nervous system, thereby enacting cardiovascular, respiratory, gastrointestinal, renal, and endocrine changes. The HPA axis, a major part of the neuroendocrine system involving the interactions of the hypothalamus, the pituitary gland, and the adrenal glands, is also activated by release of CRH and AVP.

Throughout their careers the military troops are deployed in operation and exercises both at domestic and abroad. The deployment stress dealt with physical and emotional demand relating to deployment. Both separation and reunion aspect of deployment place additional demand on family. Factor contributing to deployment are personal health, coping abilities, previous deployment experience, attitude towards the assignment, confidence in self and unit, and sense of security in family relationship. There are certain factor related to separation that may include available preparation time, previous family separation experience, attitude of family towards assignment, confidence in support available in family. The factor related to deployment are nature of mission especially if it is ambiguous, length of the mission, communication difficulties, geographical location, living and working condition, as well as confidence in unit training and leadership.

As our country's operational commitments have increased throughout the world, military Families are now often faced with deployments in more rapid succession. In many situations, it is unknown when the deployment will end, increasing the anxiety and uncertainty for military Families. Whereas the previous emotional cycles of deployment may have allowed for a period between deployments of 18 months to 2 years, some military Families are now facing another deployment of the service member within 9-12 months of the member's return. Some of the military services describe 7 stages of the emotional cycles of deployment named Anticipation of Departure; Detachment and Withdrawal, Emotional Disorganization, Recovery and Stabilization, Anticipation of Return, Return

Adjustment and Renegotiation as well as Reintegration and Stabilization.

In the anticipation of departure the military personnel may alternately feel denial and anticipation of loss. As reality sinks in, tempers may flare as couples attempt to take care of all the items on a Family pre-deployment checklist, while striving to make time for "memorable" moments. In detachment and withdrawal stage service members become more and more psychologically prepared for deployment, focusing on the mission and their unit. Bonding with their fellow service members is essential to unit cohesion, but this may create emotional distance within the marriage. Sadness and anger occur as couples attempt to protect themselves from the hurt of separation. In the new emotional cycles of deployment, as this stage happens more often and more frequently, marital problems may escalate. When a husband or wife must repeatedly create emotional "distance", they may gradually shut down their emotions. In emotional disorganization one might think that this stage of adjusting to new responsibilities and being alone would get easier. Although a military spouse may be familiar with the routine, she may also be experiencing "burn-out" and fatigue from the last deployment, and feel overwhelmed at starting this stage again. Recovery and stabilization increased confidence and a positive outlook. The anticipation of return stage is generally a happy and hectic time spent preparing for the return for the service member. In the Return Adjustment and Renegotiation stage couples and families must reset their expectations and renegotiate their roles during this stage.

The key to successful adjustment and renegotiation is open communication. Families also need to be prepared to deal with the effects of combat stress on the returning service member. Such stress and trauma can be difficult to deal with. Troops with combat stress are often irritable, guarded, and want to be alone. Some may use increased alcohol or drugs in a failed attempt to "numb" the emotional pain they are experiencing. In reintegration and stabilization stage combat stress can severely disrupt the stabilization process. Reintegration and stabilization can hit more roadblocks when a family must make a permanent change of station (PCS) move immediately upon the return of the service member. The life of military personnel is affected with various issues. For example Legal issues dealt with will, power of attorney, power of guardian, and life insurance. The Financial issues dealt with budget, accounts, investment, allotments, and income tax. The health issues dealt with medical related problem. The home issues dealt with mortgage, utility, and security.

Stress and stress injuries may contribute to misconduct in service members in general and military personnel in particular. The troop who test positive for mental health problems are twice likely to engage in un-ethical behaviour such as insulting and injuring non-combatant and loss to properties (Terri, & Lisa, 2008). They include heightened risk of suicide, post-traumatic stress disorder (PTSD), substance abuse and family violence. Common health conditions confronted by the soldiers are physical issues, psychological issues, social issues like work and families and e.g. one lacs veteran of Persian Gulf war nearly 20 year ago have reported chronic muscle pain, 37% had mental health problems; 22% reported PTSD and 17% as depression. As early in 1919 efforts were made to assess psychological conditions of combat veteran of World War-I known as shell shock those were suffering from symptoms of fatigue and anxiety. There appeared a war invisible wounds those dramatically improved with treatment. In Afghanistan and Iraq psychological and neurological injuries was very high. Department of defense has taken serious step for such psychological injuries. Military interventions must have a component that focuses on the disarmament, demobilization, and reintegration of former combatants. So, the social factors are quite influential that affect their wellbeing.

SOCIAL THEORY

The main objective of social theory (Banton, Clifford, Erosh, Lousada & Rosenthal, 1985, Jones & Moon, 1987) is to understand how social or society enters into the life of an individual and construct him socially. This theory identifies three linked practices important in this process. The first is economic practice, second is political practice and the third is ideological practice. Moreover, the social theory reveals that people are subject to economic, political and ideological forces, which are more powerful than other conscious factors affecting individuals. It also talks about the process of Subjectification refer to a dual function of "socialist therapy". First, it aims to reveal the individual, the way she/he is subject to unconscious forces and the second aim is to pursue the analysis of these forces until their social determinants are uncovered. In this way distinguishing characteristic of social therapeutic practice is to work out the structure of power relations in the individual power relations to Self-control. Furthermore, those power relationships would determine the need for change and how that change can be brought out.

This theory also distinguishes 'remembered' and 'real' community. It is through remembered community that the contradictions and antagonisms develop inside the individual. The 'remembered community' reflects a paradigm of community life that is reinforced or strengthened through media, politicians and welfare workers. The structure of the state also influences community in various ways. On this basis the distinction or classifications are made between rich and poor, different classes or castes. The control of the state extends to an extent that there is virtually management of subjectivity through mental health industry. This theory calls for development of real community alternative, which involves various processes of socialization, in which socio-economic process is one of them.

RESERVE CAPACITY MODEL

Considerable research has indicated that socioeconomic status (SES) has a powerful influence on health. The association is monotonic and the individuals with lower SES show greater vulnerability to diverse cause of morbidity and mortality when compared with their high SES counterparts. The socio-economic status appears to shape health through varied both ways, including health, behaviors, physiological mechanisms, environmental conditions, access to health care and psychological factors.

This model asserts that lower the socioeconomic status environments faster or greater will be he exposure to stress, which in turn, elicits more negative and less positive emotions. In addition, lower SES environments can lead to a greater use and depletion of mitigating psychological resources as well as fewer opportunities to develop resource reserves. Resource discrepancies and changes may contribute directly to emotional distress and greater emotional reactivity to stress exhibited by individuals with low SES, subsequently, negative emotions and low positive emotions may faster deleterious health outcomes.

Substantial research has suggested that SES exhibits an inverse, typically linear association with negative emotions and emotional disorders. In part this relationship may reflect variation in stress exposure attributable to socioeconomic environments. Nonetheless, some research has suggested that even after accounting for stressful experiences, individuals with lower SES report more emotional distress than their higher SES counterparts.

The model emphasizes towards the role of material, social and personal resources in determining psychological and other stress consequences. When faced losses as well as an inability to gather additional resources may ensure, fostering loss spirals and escalating damage, tangible and financial reserves as well as social and personal assets. The loss of resilience or mental health may be due to use reserve for coping with stress. A similar analysis has been applied directly to the observed relationship between low SES and cognitive decline related to again or diseases such as Alzheimer's. Specifically observers have suggested that the association between low educational attainment and cognitive decline is not simply due to fact that less educated people have lower mental abilities throughout their lives but that education encourages the development of a set of reserves that allows more efficient processing or develops compensatory processes to protect against age related decrements in functioning. Further, attachment processes is associated with psychological vulnerabilities and resilience.

ATTACHMENT THEORY

Childs internalization of relationship with an attachment figure create a secure base of support and comfort in time of distress and facilitates the child's exploration of widest world (Ainsworth, 1989; Bowlby, 1969, 1973, 1980, 1982). Recent theories have suggested this relational process as the circle of security (Marvin, Cooper, Hoffman & Powell, 2002) in which a Childs move from secure base to exploration and then back to safe heaven following a rupture. Contemporary theory and research recognize the interconnection between attachment, care giving, and exploration for adults (Freeney & Collins, 2004; George & Solomon, 1999).

Similar to child's adult attachment system is activated in times stress or novelty and adult turn to their attachment figure to alleviate this distress and regulate their affect (Hazan, Gur-Yaish & Campa, 2004). Bowlby and Ainsworth further proposed that young children internalize early attachment processes as internal working models of attachment which serves as relational templates with continuity throughout the life span (Hesse, 1999; Fonagy, 2001). Ultimately adult navigates their relational world influenced by either secure or insecure internal working model developed in their early work. Secure adult attachment relations are characterized by the capacity to relate to others in mutual reciprocal manners to provide coherent narratives about relationships, and to sustain continuity of connections (Basham & Miehls, 2004; Hesse, 1999).

Further Fisher and Crandle (1977) suggest that couples who are securely attached "shift freely between the dependent and depended upon position" with an open expression of need for comfort and contact as well as an open reception of that contact. In other words the attachment system of secure adult partners can be appropriately activated and de-activated in a flexible manner depends on the emotional need of an individual at any given time. In contrast insecure individual may be dismissing, pre-occupied or unresolved/disorganized in their state of mind about attachment (Hesse, 1999). It leads them towards bi-directionality, flexibility or mutuality common among secure partner. Recent research suggest that adult couples may create way of relating that are specific to the relationship and perhaps different from individuals global model of attachment or state of mind about early childhood attachment relationship.

CONCEPT OF PSYCHOLOGICAL WELLBEING

The phrase psychological well-being arose in a regulatory, rather than scientific, context thereby is a hypothetical construct whose validity can be determined only in relation to a theory that defines its properties and relation to empirical data that address the fit between predicted and observed phenomena. We do not have a theory to guide thinking and research on well-being; the development of a coherent theory of psychological well-being is an obvious research need. Such a theory ought to incorporate cognitive, behavioral, and physiological characteristics of the organism in an integrated view of well-being. It also ought to encompass the possibility of species, age, sex, and individual differences in responsiveness to the same immediate environmental situation. Some of the work that has been done so far in this domain is based on notions of how humans behave and how they react to environmental situations. Thus most of the article refers to a person with "psychological well being "as a happy, satisfied person, "while seem to be a rather than technical definition, it seems to fit every instance to find. Its utility will depend upon this relationship and a network of relationship with other (Verma & Verma, 1989).

The family stress theory (Drummet, Coleman, & Cable. (2003).; McCubbin, Joy, Cauble, Comeau, Paterson, & Needle (1980) highlight the potential influence of each family members perception and reaction life stressor on the entire families process of adapting to military related stressors such as frequent re-location and threat of deployment. The broader literature on stress and coping (Lazarus & Folkman, 1984) suggest that the accumulation of life stressor and demand faced by today's highly military families may affect their ability to cope with these stressors and in-turn result in maladjustment (McCubbin & Patterson, 1982), and affect wellbeing. However, Rutter (1993) posited a stress inoculation model to describe the process by which successful adaptation to small stressor can enhance resilience to subsequent challenges. Small challenges faced by military youths such as frequent residential moves and school transition may actually bolster their ability to adapt to other stressors such as parental deployment, and maintain their psychological resilience.

Psychological well-being seems to be whole array of biological and social, psychological changes with the passage of time and interaction with the environment, affecting its survival and adjustment potency. It is tremendously varied and complex field that involves four radical aspects of varying degrees of discreteness and overlap. These may be called the "biological" the "psychological", the "sociological", and the "socio- psychological" or behavioral". The descriptions are as follows:-

1. **Biological Aspect:** *Biologist regards the normal psychological well being as a complex of changes in cellular composition such as neuromuscular system. According to the biological aspects the health is the crucial feature in the psychological well being of an individual that has its impact on the individual's Self-image and personality and the reaction of society.*
2. **Psychological Aspect:** *It deals with the changes in sensory processes, per up that capacities, psychomotor performance, mental functioning, and so on. Psychologists are also concerned with the changes in personality and behavior of the changing individual. Attention has been given to the external influences, such as cultural expectations and environmental factors.*

3. **Sociological Aspects:** *It focuses on the changes in the individual that are characterized by changing situation of the individual as a member of the family, community and society. These include competition of many roles like, social support, demand of society, role limitation, socio-economic status, income, etc. This social content encompasses the family and friends at the level, and the society or cultural another level. The social frame- work determines the meaning of the psychological well being for the individual and social concepts, positive and negative affects.*
4. **Behavioral Aspect:** *It is concerned with the meaning the individual ascribe to the changes and internal and external adjustments he makes to them. These include inner relation with regard to such matter as changing self image, feeling, mental being, and tolerance to stress. More appropriately the psychological well-being dealt with balanced positive and negative affects.*

MODELS OF PSYCHOLOGICAL WELLBEING

There are various models of psychological wellbeing. Some of the models are as follows:-

Affect Related Model of Psychological Well-being

A model of psychological wellbeing developed by Bradburn and Caplovitz (1965) dealt with the individual position on two independent dimensions- one of the positive affect and the other is negative affect. The model specifies that an individual will be high in psychological well being in the degree to which he has an excess of +ve over -ve affect and will be low in well being in the degree to which -ve affect predominated over +ve affect. Thus in many respect , the model is similar to older pleasure pain or utility models that view an individual's happiness or well being in terms of the degree to which pleasure predominates over pain in his life experiences. This particular model stems from an empirical base. It suggests that there is a series of forces whose absence merely results in a lowering of absence of positive affect rather than any change in negative affect. On the other hand, there is also a series of different circumstances that contribute to the presence or absence of negative affect but have no influence on a person's positive affect. Since an individual's overall sense of well-being is dependent upon the relative balance of these two sets of forces, those contribute to either positive or negative affect in order to understand an individual's position along the resultant dimension of well-being.

The model proposed here for the understanding of psychological well-being is similar to one Herzberg, Mausner, and Snyderman (1959) work satisfaction. They noted the existence of one group of factors that played a role as "dissatisfies" and another group that played a role as "satisfiers". The presence of such things as low pay, poor work conditions, and disagreement with the boss led to job satisfaction. Negative affect appears too related primarily to the variables that have been dealt with by the traditional "mental- illness" approaches as compared to the positive affects that is related to the positive approach.

The fact that there are two independent dimensions then might well help us explain the differential effect of what appear to be equal amounts of stress on different individuals. Of the stress works toward changing the levels of negative affect, its total impact on well-being would be a differential function of the individual's level of positive affect. Since life is an ongoing, dynamic process, we would expect that factors affecting both positive and negative experiences are continually changing and that one's sense of well-being at any particular time might be thought of as a running average of the relative strength of positive and negative affect averaged out over the recent past.

One of the well-established findings in social science is that individuals of lower education and income are less likely to be involved in their environment and generally lead more restricted lives. Since environmental participation and variability appear to be highly related to the presence of positive affect, we would expect there to be less positive affect among lower socioeconomic groups and negative affect in the low socioeconomic status person. Of, in addition, there is a differential in terms of the difficulties in role adjustments related to negative affect, we would expect an even stronger relationship between socioeconomic status and overall well-being. It is important to note, however, that even without such differential difficulties in coping with problems; we would expect differences in well-being due to the restrictions on environmental variability and social participation that are characteristics of lower socioeconomic groups.

The use of psychological well-being as the major dependent variable that focuses on interpersonal problems, negative affect, social participation, sociability, environmental variability, and factors that appears to be more related to positive affect and to be concern of those oriented toward positive mental health. This conception offers a model that enables each type of study to contribute to an understanding of the basic phenomenon of psychological well being

Social Cognitive Theory

This theory was formulated by Albert Bandura (1961, 1977, 1986, 2001, and 2004). Basic purpose of social cognitive theory was to understand and predict individual and group behaviour; to identify methods in which behaviour can be modified or changed and to use intervention aimed at personality development, behaviour pathology and health promotion. The theory defines human behaviour as triadic, dynamic, and reciprocal interaction of personal, behaviour and the environmental factors. It contends that behaviour is largely regulated antecedently through the cognitive processes.

In reciprocal determinism there is interaction between environment, personal factors and behaviour. The symbolizing capability dealt with most external influences that affect behaviour through cognitive processes and the symbols (e.g. images or mental pictures or words) serve as the mechanism for thought. Vicarious processes refer to human ability to learn not only from direct experience but also from the observation of others. Forethought is a person's capability to motivate them and guide their action anticipatorily (Bandura, 1989). A self-regulatory system is an internal control mechanism that governs what behaviour is performed and the self-imposed consequences for that behaviour. The self-reflective capability enables people to analyze their experiences, think about their own thought processes, and alter their thinking accordingly (Bandura, 1986, 2001, 2004). Therefore, response consequences of behaviour are used to form expectations of behavioural outcomes. It gives strong emphasis on one's cognition by suggesting that the mind is an active force that constructs one's reality, selectively encodes information, performs behaviour on the basis of value and expectations and imposes structure on its own actions. Key concept in this theory is reciprocal determinism, symbolizing capability, vicarious capability, forethought capability, self-regulatory capability and self-reflective capability.

The manner in which human agency operates has been conceptualized in at least three different ways-as autonomous agency, mechanical agency or emergent interactive agency. In the concept of agency self-referent processes are epiphenomenalism by products of conditioned responses that do not enter into the determination of action. Successful functioning requires and agentic blend of these different modes of agency (Pajares, 2002). Gandhiji also mobilizes massive collective force that bring socio political change, although lives ascetically not self-indulgently (Bandura, 2001). There involves the greater role of brain in cognitive processing upon which social cognitive theory rest.

According to Bandura (2002) culture are diverse and dynamic social system not static monoliths that exert its influence on human being.

The social cognitive theory posits that factors such as economic conditions, socioeconomic status, and educational familial structure do not affect human behaviour directly instead they influence people's aspiration, self-efficacy beliefs, personal standards, emotional states. This social cognitive theory reveals human and collective functioning as the profound influence on psychological thinking and theorizing fundamental human capabilities. Bandura (1997) regard role of self-efficacy beliefs in human functioning and told that peoples level of motivation, affective state and actions are based more on what they believe than on what is objectively true. Self- beliefs are critical ingredient in human functioning that help in determining efforts people spend in their activities. It influence thought pattern and emotional reactions.

Personal Construct Theory (PCT)

Personal Construct theory was developed by the American psychologist George Kelly in the 1950s that deals with the personality development and human cognition. It represents a coherent, comprehensive psychology of personality and cognition that has special relevance for psychotherapy. Its predominant focus remains on the study of individuals, families, and social groups, with particular emphasis on how people organize and change their views of self and the world. The theory explicitly states that each individual's psychological task is to put in order the facts of his or her own experience or constructed knowledge by performing those actions. If the results of our actions are in line with what the knowledge predicted then we have done a good job of finding the order in our personal experience. If not, then we must be willing to change our interpretations or our predictions or both. People develop constructs as internal ideas of reality in order to understand the world around them. They can be based on observations or experiences. Every construct is bipolar, specifying how two things are similar to each other (lying on the same pole) and different from a third thing. They can be expanded with new ideas.

At the base of Kelly's theory is the image of the person-as-scientist, a view that emphasizes the human capacity for meaning making, agency, and ongoing revision of personal systems of knowing across time. Thus, individuals, like incipient scientists, are seen as creatively formulating constructs, or hypotheses about the apparent regularities of their lives, in an attempt to make them understandable, and to some extent, predictable. However, predictability is not pursued for its own sake, but is instead sought as a guide to practical action in concrete contexts and relationships. This implies that people engage in continuous extension, refinement, and revision of their systems of meaning as they meet with events that challenge, or invalidate their assumptions, prompting their personal theories toward greater adequacy.

Kelly formally developed his theory through a series of corollaries, which can be broadly grouped into those concerned with the process of construing, the structure of personal knowledge, and the social embedded ness of our construing efforts. At the level of process, PCT envisions people as actively organizing their perceptions of events on the basis of recurring themes, meanings attributed to the 'booming, buzzing confusion' of life in an attempt to render it interpretable. By punctuating the unending flow of experience into coherent units, people are able to discern similarities and differences of events in terms that are both personally significant and shared by relevant others.

At the level of structure, PCT suggests that meaning is a matter of contrast - an individual attributes meaning to an event not only by construing what it is, but also by differentiating it from what it is not. It places a strong emphasis on emotional experiences, understood as signals of actual or impending transitions in one's fundamental constructs for anticipating the world. Alternatively, people might experience anxiety when confronted with events that seem almost completely alien and uninterruptible within their previous construct system. This attention to the delicate interweaving of meaning and affect has made this theory as an attractive framework for contemporary researchers and clinicians concerned with such topics as relational breakdown, trauma, and loss, all of which can fundamentally undercut one's assumptive world, triggering a host of significant emotional and behavioral responses. It attempt to set in order the facts of human experience so that the psychologist could make good predictions about what people will do when confronted by new situations.

As an approach to psychotherapy, PCT stresses the importance of the therapist making a concerted effort to enter the client's world of meaning and understand it 'from the inside out', as a precondition to assisting with its revision. In this way the therapist does not assume to be an expert who guides clients toward a more 'rational' or 'objectively true' way of thinking. Instead, he or she works to help clients recognize the coherence in their own ways of construing experience, as well as their personal agency in making modifications in these constructions when necessary.

CHAPTER

3

MILITARY LIFE AND MENTAL HEALTH

Only by actually arming ourselves mentally with Mao's thoughts can we be good and do good ceaselessly. The countless model heroes were able to perform heroic deeds of various kinds under dissimilar circumstances because they had attained a revolutionary world outlook devoted to a struggle to the finish for communism……Come ghosts or ghouls, imperialism or revisionists, they have no fear for any enemy and they hold hardship and adversity yin contempt. They can wealthier any kind of political storm and withstand the ravages of a force 12 typhoon (CFCP, 1965).

Is the concept of "human security", which has been discussed and debated in international organizations and academic circles since 1994, simply "hot air", as its critics claim? Or does it provide a suitable framework for proposing multi-sectoral, integrated solutions in a world that is increasingly interconnected? While there is no consensus as to the exact definition of the term, human security goes beyond traditional notions of security to focus on such issues as development and respect for human rights. To some the concept is attractive, but analytically weak since it introduces too many variables that are not necessarily linked together. To others, human security concerns should be limited to situations marked by the threat or outbreak of violence. For those who favor a broad definition (as does this author), the human security agenda provides the means to assess the root causes of conflict (whether intra-state or inter-state), to propose adequate policies for resolving crises, and to provide the means for sustainable peace-building. In so doing human security policies focus on social and economic issues as they affect the individual, arguing that security is dependent on a wide-ranging network of factors that require a comprehensive approach to be effective (Shahrbanou, 2010).

Some comrades take the view that modern warfare differs from warfare in the past, that since the weapons and equipment available to our army in the past were inferior we had to emphasize dependence on man, on his bravery and wisdom; in order to win victories. They say that modern warfare is a war of technique, of steel and machinery and that in the face of these things; man's role has to be relegated to a second place. They attach importance only to machinery and want to turn revolutionary soldiers into robots devoid of revolutionary initiative. Contrary to these people, we believe that while equipment and techniques are important, the human factor is even more so. Technique also has to be mastered by man. Men and material must form a unity with men as the leading factor. This was a subtle but significant modification of the theory that men are superior to material which had placed man in a position of unqualified primacy. Therefore, the deed of human beings are directly associated with their mental wellness.

MILITARY LIFE AND MENTAL HEALTH

Military families like civilian one represent diversities with single parents and binuclear households. They dealt with stressful issues like finance, child and elderly care, physical and mental challenges. Their families are unique in facing the required challenge of tolerating and adapting to the multiple deployment and family separation. Mental health and wellbeing among military personnel is important for the effectiveness of nation's military, adjustment of their families and the integration of military personnel into the larger civilian community. Well-being is generally recognized as a vital and multi-dimensional component of health in both civilian and military contexts. The World Health Organization defines health as "a state of complete physical, mental and social well-being and not merely the absence of disease or infirmity. Moreover, well-being has been identified as a critical aspect of military readiness by the recent United States Department of Defense Suicide Prevention Task Force and the current Principal Deputy under Secretary of Defense for

Personnel and Readiness. However, the concept of well-being poses challenges, including the lack of universally accepted definitions, its multi-dimensional structure, and the broad, eclectic understanding of health that it implies. This review will include a summary of 1) definitions, 2) dimensions, and 3) measures of well-being (Mark & Bowles, 2011).

According to Goldenson (1984), mental health is a state of mind, characterized by emotional well-being, relative freedom from anxiety and disabling symptoms and a capacity to establish constructive relationship with ordinary demands and stresses of life. It is more than the absence of mental illness, for the states and capacities noted in the definition has value in them. The study of Zeiss and Dickman (1989) on a statewide sample of WWII ex-PoWs(N = 442) responded to questionnaires that sampled current and past difficulties with PTSD-related symptoms; an incidence of serious difficulties with these symptoms of 56% was revealed. Retrospective reports of temporal patterns revealed no consistent patterns of symptom occurrence, but, rather, a waxing and waning of difficulties over the 40-year period. Unexpectedly, measures of severity of the POW experiences did not predict current symptomatology. Rank at time of capture, however, was consistently and strongly predictive of PTSD. It is suggested that PTSD is a highly persistent phenomenon and that both situation and person variables contribute to the development and maintenance of PTSD. The relationship of PTSD symptoms to combat exposure was examined in 1,210 Veterans of World War II (WWII) and the Korean War, who were participants in the Normative Aging Study. WWII Veterans exposed to moderate or heavy combat had 13.3 times greater risk of PTSD symptoms measured 45 years later, compared with non-combat Veterans (Spiro, Schnurr, & Aldwin 1994).

Lester (1995) examined suicide rates in association with military participation rates in France from 1850 to 1913. During periods of war, the suicide rates were lower than during periods of peace, while the Military participation rate was positively associated with the suicide rate. Despite this, mental health is still portrayed by some as a luxury. The misunderstandings on which this view is based are now clearer than they were in the past, and WHO and other international organizations identify the improvement of mental health as a priority concern for low and middle income countries as well as for wealthier nations and people (WHO, 2001b). Neither mental nor physical health can exist alone. Mental, physical and social functioning is interdependent. Furthermore, health and illness may co-exist. They are mutually exclusive only if health is defined in a restrictive way as the absence of disease (Sartorius, 1990). Ryff et al (1995), have proposed a theoretical model of well-being, which encompasses six distinct dimensions of wellness: 'autonomy', 'environment', 'mastery', 'personal growth', 'positive relation with others', 'purpose in life', and 'self-acceptance'. Subjective well-being is an important aspect of one's total health status.

Reducing failure and recycling in demanding military Advanced Individual Training (AIT) programs will reduce costs: time and morale for the soldiers and financial costs for the organization. This study is one in a series, examining factors internal and external to the soldiers that can influence performance during AIT. The purpose of this research was to document self-esteem among 253 soldiers attending health care specialist training using the Rosenberg self-esteem survey and to examine the relationship between self-esteem, general demographics, self-reported health, motivation, self-efficacy and grade point average (GPA). Self-reports of self-esteem were categorized as 11% low, 37% moderate, and 52% high. No relationship was found between self-esteem and gender, marital status. Age, race, military component or high school GPA or science grades (p>0.05). Self-esteem was significantly correlated with self-reported health, status, endurance, strength, self-efficacy and motivation. But no relationship was found between self-esteem and GPA (Rice, Butler, & Marra, 1996). Spiro, Schnurr, and Aldwin (1997) studied the positive and negative developmental effects of military service on men's aging. The study utilizes life-span approach to outline its application to the study of military service. It points out that military service is a hidden variable in men's aging, and the failure to consider its con-sequences has important implications for the understanding of aging. To illustrate some aspects of the life-span perspective they offered normative approach.

The study Schnurr, Spiro, Aldwin, and Stukel (1998) modeled physical symptom trajectories from ages 30 to 75 in 1,079 older male military Veterans who were assessed every 3 to 5 years since the 1960s. Combat exposure and noncombat trauma were used to define four groups: no trauma (N = 249), noncombat trauma only (N = 333), combat only (N = 152), and both combat and non-combat trauma (N = 345). Number of symptoms on the Cornell Medical Index physical symptom scale increased 29% per decade. Men who had experienced either combat or noncombat trauma did not differ from no exposed men, but those who had experienced both combat and noncombat trauma had 16% more symptoms across all ages. There were no differences in age-related trajectories as a function of trauma history. In cross-sectional analysis, with combat and noncombat trauma had more PTSD symptoms, but not more depression symptoms, than men with either no trauma or noncombat trauma only. Discussion focuses on the importance of considering physical as well as psychological outcomes of expo-sure to traumatic events.

The Swiss Army is currently engaged in a process of reorganization; 'Swiss Army XXI' will start in 2003 with a smaller but more efficient Army. For two years how many professional officers and civilians have been working out proposals and solutions for this project. Discussion has also focused on the recruitment process, and the Dept. of Applied Psychology of the University of Zurich was commissioned to draw up a conception concerning the psychological aspects of recruitment. The concept treats three levels: basic recruitment, assessment of leader potential and assessment of leader potential and assessment of high ranking officers. By using computer based Psychological tests such as personality questionnaires, intelligence tests, psycho-motor test batteries or tests of so: Diminishing the drop-out rate during military basic training by assessing Psychological resources. Diminishing the drop-out rate during military basic training by assessing Psychological resources. Collecting more detailed information on the conscript to establish a well-founded assignment to military functions. Obtaining a more homogenous distribution of conscript with leadership potential across different military functions. Support of the decision making process for the admission to military leadership schools through a detailed leadership related aptitude clarification. cial competence, the following goals should be attained (Patrick, B. (2000).

The military recruitment is directed associated with their health which is defined as a state of complete physical, mental and social well-being of a person not merely the absence of disease or infirmity (WHO, 2001b, p.1).Three ideas central to the improvement of health follow from this definition: mental health is an integral part of health, therefore is more than the absence of mental illness, and is intimately connected with physical health and behaviour. Defining mental health is important, although not always necessary for achieving its improvement. Differences in values across countries, cultures, classes and genders can appear too great to allow a consensus on a definition (WHO, 2001c). However, just as age or wealth each have many different expressions across the world and yet have a core common-sense universal meaning, so too can be understood without restricting its interpretation across cultures. WHO has recently proposed that mental health is a state of well-being in which the individual realizes his or her own abilities, can cope with the normal stresses of life, can work productively and fruitfully, and is able to make a contribution to his or her community (WHO, 2001, p.1). In this positive sense, mental health is the foundation for well-being and effective functioning for an individual and for a community. Similarly

, the study of Port, Engdahl, Frazier and Eberly (2002) examined the relationships between socio environmental factors occurring in later life and current and changing PTSD symptom levels in a sample of 177 community-dwelling World War II and Korean era ex-prisoners of war. Factors examined included negative life events, negative health events, social support, and death acceptance. PTSD was assessed at Time 1. PTSD and the later-life factors were then assessed 4 years later (Time 2). Cross-sectional analysis examined the relationship of the later-life factors to current PTSD symptomatology. Longitudinal analysis examined their relationship to changing PTSD symptomatology over the 4 year interval. Negative health changes, social support, and death acceptance were significantly related to current and changing PTSD symptomatology, but negative life events were not. The authors conclude that health and psychosocial factors that may occur in later life can be related to PTSD symptom levels even many decades after a traumatic experience. Such symptoms can be linked with various paradigms.

The recovery model as it applies to mental health is an approach to mental disorder or substance dependence (and/or from being labeled in those terms) that emphasizes and supports each individual's potential for recovery. Recovery is seen within the model as a personal journey, that may involve developing hope, a secure base and sense of self, supportive relationships, empowerment, social inclusion, coping skills, and meaning. Originating from the 12-Step Program of Alcoholics Anonymous and the Civil Rights Movement, the use of the concept in mental health emerged as deinstitutionalization resulted in more individuals living in the community. It gained impetus due to a perceived failure by services or wider society to adequately support social inclusion, and by studies demonstrating that many can recover. This model is now been explicitly adopted as the guiding principle of the mental health systems of a number of countries and states. In many cases practical steps are being taken to base services on the recovery model, although there are varieties of obstacles and concerns raised. A number of standardized measures have been developed to assess aspects of recovery, although there is some variation between professionalized models and those originating in the Psychiatric survivors movement. The mental health now ranks as a priority within the international health and development agenda. Governments across the world and health professionals across the disciplines are now more aware of the importance of mental health issues to the overall health of individuals, communities, cities, and even entire nations (Herrman, Saxena & Moodie, 2005).The Impact of Armed Violence on poverty and development was assessed by the Centre for International Cooperation and Security Department of Peace (2005) in order to document the relationship which DFID feels is widely accepted but not confirmed. This report synthesizes the findings of 13 country case studies. In addition it has a practical policy-oriented purpose and concludes with programming and policy recommendations to donor government agencies.

The study conducted by Kang, Bullman, & Taylor, (2006) evaluated healthcare utilization data for 10 years (1991-2000) from Veterans Affairs (VA) and non-VA health-care *providers for 19,442 former WWII PoWs and 9,728 non-PoW controls. The risk of diseases was approximated by odds ratios adjusted for race and age. Results revealed that former POWs had statistically significant increased risk of PTSD, and those PoWs with PTSD also had statistically significant increased risks of cardiovascular diseases including hypertension and chronic ischemic heart disease when compared to both non-POWs and POWs without PTSD. Conclusions: Among former WWII PoWs, risk of cardiovascular disease is related to having PTSD. Further, Bramsen, Deeg, Van der Ploeg, and Fransman (2007) studied late-life mortality among 1,448 World War II survivors. The highest hazard rates of mortality were found among military Veterans and war survivors who had been seriously wounded. PTSD, suicidal thoughts, and depression were associated with a higher hazard rate. Sixty four supervisors in three selected military hospitals in Tehran have been studied in a descriptive epidemiological study via cross-sectional method. A researcher- made questionnaire was applied to collect the data. The validity and reliability of the questionnaire were proved by the experts and Cronbach's alpha (r=0.90), respectively. Both descriptive and analytical tests such as ANOVA were employed to analyze the data. On the basis of the findings more than 51percent of the subjects were male, 84.4% had a B.Sc. degree and more than 87% were married. With regard to the underlined issue, 50% of the applicants were educated about hospital infectious and more than 54% attended in related Seminars. The differences among supervisors' knowledge in the studied hospitals were statistically significant (p< 0.05). More than 64% of the study* *population, in general, was good informed with respect to hospital infectious (Ahmad, Reza, Hormoz, & Aliakbar, 2007).*

America seems to have moved to a position in history where we are captivated with thoughts of military power. Not since World War II has America been engaged in combat along two theaters of combat operation - Iraq and Afghanistan. We now have extended our military prowess and declared war against global terrorism, which means the number of potential combat front lines is impossible to determine. The initial blowback from such a strategy seems to be an economic catastrophe at home. This article focuses on another potential blowback - an emerging storm that encompasses the war at home that Afghanistan and Iraq Veterans are beginning to experience. The lessons from the aftermath of the Vietnam are available for all to review. A disinterest acknowledging those lessons seems to be prevailing. This article is written as evidence for the men and women who serve, or have served, in Afghanistan and Iraq that they have support for their second war - the war that begins when they leave the military. This article also challenges researchers and service providers to begin preparation to support these veterans (William, 2008). The study of Ikin, Sim, McKenzie, Horsley, Wilson, Harrex, et al. (2009) aimed to examine life satisfaction and quality of life in Australia's surviving male Korean War Veterans and a community comparison group, and to investigate any association with war deployment-related factors. Methods: Participants completed a postal questionnaire which included the Life Satisfaction Scale, the brief World Health Organization Quality of Life (WHOQOL-Bref) questionnaire, *and the Combat Exposure Scale. Resultsrevealed that Korean War Veterans reported significantly lower Percentage Life Satisfaction (PLS) and quality of life scores on four WHOQOL-Bref domains, compared with similarly aged Australian men (each p value <0.001). These outcomes were most strongly associated with severity of combat exposure and low rank. Mean PLS was approximately 15% lower in Veterans who reported heavy combat compared with those reporting no combat, and approximately 12% lower in enlisted ranked Veterans compared with officers.*

Job satisfaction and occupational stress both indicate workers' appraisal towards the workplace and work itself. Thus, it is important to have valid measure of job satisfaction and occupational stress. This measure is also important in the Malaysian workplace context. A total of 40 male officers and non-officers, from the seaman and engineering and supply branch in the Lumut Naval Base participated in the study. Data were collected using a self-administered questionnaire, the Job Satisfaction Survey (Spector, 1985) and Job Related Tension Index (JRTI; Kahn et al., 1964). This preliminary study established internal consistency using Cronbach alpha values for both instruments. Additionally, the study determined the level of occupational stress, job satisfaction and relationship between occupational stress and job satisfaction facets. The findings of the study revealed that the reliability of both instruments were greater than 0.80. The majority of the male Navy personnel reported moderate levels of job satisfaction in the favorable nature of work facet. High occupational stress on the other hand, was related to an unknown superior's evaluation of one's workplace performance. Correlational analyses found that occupational stress was associated with overall job satisfaction and in eight of its facets. Collectively, results provide evidence that both instruments are reliable in the Malaysian military setting context. Caution should be made that finding of this preliminary study should not be generalized to the larger population due to its small sample size. A bigger sample would be needed to represent the general population (Mansor, 2009).

A careful examination of psychological issues confronting military personnel must necessarily be broaden in scope that may include a range of discipline within psychology and social sciences to provide a comprehensive assessment of the factor that affect the performance, health and wellbeing of military personnel and their families. Such multi-disciplinary approaches ensures researches military readers policy makers and health care provider with a framework for understanding key factors relevant to modern military operations (Britt, Adler & Andrew, 2010). Aim of the study was to assess long lasting effect of ethnic conflict on health and wellbeing. Further risk factors for victimization during the conflict and factor contributing to healing. Cross-sectional survey was conducted on 1115 household with a population of 6845 interview were carried out. Result revealed that over 90% of families had been exposed to at least two categories of violence and human right violation, and 493 individuals from 341 families reported torture experience. Further 20% people suffered from physical and mental pain. The effect of ethnic conflict on health and well-being was not found. The level of lifetime exposure to violence, the proportion of family members reporting pain and lifetime violence related injury and families financial burden were found to be inter-correlated (Wang, Salihu, Rushiti, Bala & Modwig, 2010).

The relationships between life satisfaction and the severity of the injuries were examined using interview data collected in a follow-up study of soldiers who received penetrating head wounds during the war in Lebanon in 1982-1985. Mean reported life satisfaction in the past was higher than that noted immediately after injury, following rehabilitation or for the future, while the lowest levels of satisfaction were reported around the time of injury. Post rehabilitation satisfaction was higher than that recorded immediately after the injury, and there was a consistent tendency for reporting aspirations for higher satisfaction in the future. Life satisfaction was highly correlated with education and being married but not with age or the patients' severity of injury. The residual disability was directly related to life satisfaction; with the more seriously affected having lower scores. Those who returned to service had higher satisfaction scores compared to those who could not or did not want to return to active military service. There were lower satisfaction scores for those with existential or aesthetic anxiety. Life satisfaction is suggested as an important measure of the success of rehabilitation (Linn, Linn, Segal, Sheps, Levi, & Revach, 2011).

DEPLOYMENT CYCLE AND WELL-BEING

The deployment cycle definitely can be associated with the psychological wellbeing of the person especially in the personnel serving the Military. More than 1.6 million military men and women have deployed to fight the global war on terror. Although studies have suggested that approximately one third of these service men and women return with a mental health condition or a brain injury, a gap remains in our understanding about how these individuals cope with and grow from their experiences. Older studies of Vietnam Veterans demonstrate the negative impact on families of war-related PTSD. These Veterans have higher levels of marital problems, family violence, and partner distress. Their children present more behavioral problems than do those of Veterans without PTSD. Veterans with the highest levels of symptomology had families with the worst functioning (Kulka, Schlenger, Fairbank, Hough, Jordan, Marmar, et al. (1990).

Deployment and duty related separation can be defined on the spectrum that includes schedules training exercises or mission, planned peacekeeping rotations, overseas tour of duty, and combat. The duration deployment and duty related separation can typically range from several weeks to one year. Military separation is a defining part of military life that is experienced by most of military personnel and their family. Military deployment and duty related separation are defining experience for military services member and their families. They are one of the most widely recognized and documented stressors for military families. They also impact the military mission and influence service member retention (Albano, 1994; Black, 1993; Drumet, Coleman & Cable, Kelly et al, 2001; Orthner, 2002; Orthner, Bowen, & Beare, 1990; Vormbrock, 1993). Nevertheless, the separation can also strengthened military couples and families' resilience because of peacetime and war families are crucial to the wellbeing and effectiveness of military personnel.

Hall and Jansen (1995) evaluated 47 commissioned officers, 86 noncommissioned officers, and 92 juniors enlisted soldiers from the 28th combat support Hospital for stress and arousal during deployment preparations for operation up hold democracy. Increased levels of arousal were found in officers and older soldiers. Higher levels of arousal were also found in subjects reporting a greater numbers of hours of sleep during the preceding 24 hours. No significant difference was found in stress scores for several demographic and coping behavior groups. Lower arousal scores suggest that younger, sleep deprived, and enlisted soldiers may be at the highest risk for accidents during deployment preparations. Kashes, (1996) reviewed the basic principles of the management of stress reactions in the combat setting, with an emphasis on the need for continuation of care to prevent long-term effects. Modalities for managing returning soldiers, focusing on an impatient setting, and indicate directions for further research. Historical overview of psychological injury and readjustment, treatment of battle fatigue, returning home, treatment (specific treatments, assessment and diagnosis, development of treatment plans, complications), reintegration, unique factors in the Persian Gulf War. Lerner, Y. & Zilber, N. (1996) studied 328 immigrants to Israel from the former Soviet Union. The sc (who had already been screened for Psychological/ Psychiatric Epidemiology Research Interview. Psychological symptoms during the war were associated with pre-war level of distress and with actual physical harm from the missiles, but not with exposure to danger; correlates of behavior in the face of life-threatening danger during the war were also identified. Overall the level of postwar psychological distress was not higher than prewar levels, which may be explained by the Ss' feelings of shared fate, belonging and sense of cohesion, which characterize the general Israeli population during war time.

The numbing and avoidance experienced by Veterans with PTSD is associated with lower parenting satisfaction.(14) The difficulty these Veterans have experiencing emotions and their sense of detachment may make it difficult for them in their personal relationships, and may even lead to behavioral problems on the part of their children. More recent studies of personnel deployed to Afghanistan and Iraq have looked at family functioning in the near-term post-deployment period. In one study, soldiers' dissociative symptoms, sexual problems, and sleep disturbances had the greatest impact on relationships. The total number of traumatic events experienced, either during the war or in other contexts, did not significantly affect relationship satisfaction.(15) In a sample referred for mental health evaluation, 75% of Veterans with partners reported at least one family adjustment issue. Fifty four percent of these Veterans reported shouting with, shoving or pushing current or former partners. Symptoms of depression were associated with family problems generally and domestic abuse in particular. Among Veterans with children, those with more severe PTSD and depression were more likely to report that their children were afraid of them or lacked warmth towards them.

The current combat operations in Iraq and Afghanistan have involved U.S. military personnel in major ground combat and hazardous security duty. Studies are needed to systematically assess the mental health of members of the armed services who have participated in these operations and to inform policy with regard to the optimal delivery of mental health care to returning veterans. The researchers studied members of four U.S. combat infantry units (three Army units and one Marine Corps unit) using an anonymous survey that was administered to the subjects either before their deployment to Iraq (n=2530) or three to four months after their return from combat duty in Iraq or Afghanistan (n=3671). The outcomes included major depression, generalized anxiety, and post-traumatic stress disorder (PTSD), which were evaluated on the basis of standardized, self-administered screening instruments. Exposure to combat was significantly greater among those who were deployed to Iraq than among those deployed to Afghanistan. The percentage of study subjects whose responses met the screening criteria for major depression, generalized anxiety, or PTSD was significantly higher after duty in Iraq (15.6 to 17.1 percent) than after duty in Afghanistan (11.2 percent) or before deployment to Iraq (9.3 percent); the largest difference was in the rate of PTSD. Of those whose responses were positive for a mental disorder, only 23 to 40 percent sought mental health care. Those whose responses were positive for a mental disorder were twice as likely as those whose responses were negative to report concern about possible stigmatization and other barriers to seeking mental health care (Charles, Carl, Stephen, Dennis, Dave, & Robert L. 2004).

Fiedler, Ozakinci, Hallman, Wartenberg, Brewer, Barrett, and Kiepen (2006) found military deployment to the gulf war as a risk factor for psychiatric illness among us troop. Interview data from 967 Gulf War Veteran and 784 Era Veteran were examined to determine current health status, medical conditions, and symptom that logistic regression model has verified. Result revealed that the gulf war veteran had significantly higher prevalence of psychiatric diagnosis, with twice the prevalence of anxiety disorder and depression. Lower rank, female gender, and divorced or single married status were significantly independent predictor of psychiatric disorder. Therefore the deployment of gulf war was associated with range of mental health outcomes more than after ten year after deployment.

After injuries in the war the military personnel has to undergo with various psychological trauma such as incontinence and impotence social difficulties or social assets problems. For example the literature on sexuality after injury has its impact on sexual functioning and reproductive functioning sexual behaviour and adjustment thereof their health (Hugh & de Girolambo, 2007). Veteran of operation enduring freedom and Iraqi freedom have endured high combat stress and are eligible for two year of free military service related health care yet little known about their mental health. Out of 103738 veteran seen at health care facilities, 25658 (25%) received mental health diagnosis; 56% of whom had or more distinct mental health diagnosis. Overall 32010 (31%) received mental health services and/or psychological diagnosis. Younger groups were more prone towards receiving mental health services (Seal, Bertenthal, Miner, Sen,

& Marmar, 2007). The study of Jose, Donald, and Mark (2007) provides a framework for considering the global burden of illness attributable to dengue, and its cost, and describes challenges encountered in the estimation of these values. Major challenges include: lack of uniform application of the World Health Organization (WHO) case definition, limited capabilities and standards of dengue laboratories, limited accuracy of rapid tests, misdiagnosis, lack of uniform criteria to report cases of dengue to WHO, limited role of surveillance and reporting systems, under-reporting of fatal and non-fatal dengue, misclassification in reporting, limited public knowledge about major regions at risk and travellers. While the scientific literature contains few studies on the burden of dengue and cost of illness, available results suggest that the actual number of cases of dengue may range from 3 to 27 times the reported number.

By the end of 2008, 1.7 million American service members had served in Operation Enduring Freedom and Operation Iraqi Freedom (OEF/OIF).(1) Military personnel serving in Iraq and Afghanistan run the risk of developing problems such as depression, PTSD, anxiety, and traumatic brain injury due to their deployment. Studies of these returning service members and Veterans have found rates of 4% to 14% for depression, 12% to 25% for PTSD, 11% to 19% for traumatic brain injury, and 18% to 35% for any mental health risk or concern(Mental Health Advisory Team , 2008; Milliken, Auchterlonie, & Hoge, 2007; Tanielin, & Jaycox, 2008). Forty-three percent of active duty service members have children. These children face the challenges inherent in having a parent deployed. Many of them must also cope with living with a parent who returns profoundly changed by war. Most families will be able to overcome these adversities through the support of family, friends, and community. Others, however, will need additional help from service providers to strengthen their resilience, access needed services, and readjust to life post-deployment. Veterans themselves recognize the need for such services. In a recent study of Veterans receiving treatment for PTSD, nearly 80% were interested in greater family involvement in their care

To compare the prevalence and intensity of posttraumatic stress disorder (PTSD) among Kuwaiti military men, divided into four groups (50 subjects each) according to degree of exposure to war trauma: (1) the retired (retired before the invasion); (2) an active-in-the-army group (AIA) (involved in duties at the rear only); (3) an in-battle (IB) group (involved in combat); and (4) prisoners of war (POWs-captured during combat). Second, to compare the severity of impact of event, co morbid depression, and anxiety among the groups. Third, to evaluate the contribution of self-esteem and locus of control (LOC). Subjects were interviewed once, 6 years after the war, using: the Clinician Administered PTSD Scale; the Impact of Event Scale (IES); the Hopkins Symptom Checklist-25; the Internal-External LOC; and The Self-Esteem Scale. Subjects were aged 24-71 years (mean 37.9). Sixty-three subjects (31.5%) fulfilled criteria for PTSD, with the rate significantly higher among the POWs (48%) than the retired (24%) and IB (22%), reflecting the severity of IES. Avoidance symptoms were the most pronounced. Self-esteem was significantly lowest among the POWs and those with PTSD. External LOC was associated with PTSD, anxiety, and depression. Self-esteem was the only covariate of PTSD scores. LOC was a significant covariate for anxiety. The characteristics of PTSD in these veterans showed similarity with those from elsewhere. The prominence of self-esteem and avoidance symptoms implies that they should be part of focus for interventions. Focus on LOC should be from the perspective of anxiety (Al-Turkait, & Ohaeri, 2008).

The study of Chandra and Martin (2009) observed that military families have experienced multiple and extended deployments. Little is known about the effect of parental deployment on the well-being of children, and few, if any, studies to date have engaged school staff to understand whether and how parental deployments affect the behavioral, social, and emotional outcomes of youth in the school setting. Focus groups and semi-structured interviews were conducted with teachers, counselors, and administrative staff at schools serving children from U.S. Army families. Participants were queried about the academic, behavioral, and emotional issues faced by children of deployed soldiers. Data were analyzed for themes in these areas, with attention to differences by service component (Active Component vs. Army Reserve and National Guard). Results revealed that although some children seem to be coping well with deployment, school staff felt that children's anxiety related to parental absence, increased responsibilities at home, poor mental health of some no deployed parents, and difficulty accessing mental health services affected the ability of other students to function well in school. Forty-three percent of active duty service members have children. (ICF International Demographics 2007). These children face the challenges inherent in having a parent deployed. Many of them must also cope with living with a parent who returns profoundly changed by war. Most families will be able to overcome these adversities through the support of family, friends, and community. Others, however, will need additional help from service providers to strengthen their resilience, access needed services, and readjust to life post-deployment. Veterans themselves recognize the need for such services. In a recent study of Veterans receiving treatment for PTSD, nearly 80% were interested in greater family involvement in their care. (Batten, Drapalski, Decker, DeViva, Morris, Mann et al., 2009)0. Veterans of various service eras (N=174) completed a survey about combat exposure, PTSD symptoms, depression, guilt and meaning in life. Results of a hierarchical regression indicated that younger age; higher levels of combat exposure, depression, & guilt; and lower meaning in life predicted greater PTSD severity. The interaction between meaning in life and depression also was significant, with a stronger inverse relation between meaning and PTSD at lower levels of depression. Meaning in life may be an important treatment concern for veterans with PTSD symptoms, particularly at higher levels of functioning (Owens, Steger, Whitesell & Herrera, 2009).

Sudin, Fear, HullJones, Dandekar, Hotof, Wessely, and Rona (2010) conducted their research in order to know how individual perceive their deployment experience and subsequently feel positive and negative stress. The study was conducted on 5573 UK military personnel who had deployed in Iraq during 2003 and 2006. Association between deployment and health was examined. Result revealed that deployment was related to military task such as doing the job you were trained to do as well as altruistic aspect i.e. to help the people. The unrewarding aspects were being separated from family and friends. Those with psychological problem found deployment and coalition with forces as unrewarding.

Military operations in Iraq and Afghanistan have involved the frequent and extended deployment of military personnel, many of whom are married. The effect of deployment on mental health in military spouses is largely unstudied. The study examined electronic medical-record data for outpatient care received between 2003 and 2006 by 250,626 wives of active-duty U.S. Army soldiers. After adjustment for the socio-demographic characteristics and the mental health history of the wives, as well as the number of deployments of the personnel, we compared mental health diagnoses according to the number of months of deployment in Operation Iraqi Freedom in the Iraq-Kuwait region and Operation Enduring Freedom in Afghanistan during the same period. The deployment of spouses and the length of deployment were associated with mental health diagnoses. In adjusted analyses, as compared with wives of personnel who were not deployed, women whose husbands were deployed for 1 to 11 months received more diagnoses of depressive disorders (27.4 excess cases per 1000 women; 95% confidence interval [CI], 22.4 to 32.3), sleep disorders (11.6 excess cases per 1000; 95% CI, 8.3 to 14.8), anxiety (15.7 excess cases per 1000; 95% CI, 11.8 to 19.6), and acute stress reaction and adjustment disorders (12.0 excess cases per 1000; 95% CI, 8.6 to 15.4). Deployment for more than 11 months was associated with 39.3 excess cases of depressive disorders (95% CI, 33.2 to 45.4), 23.5 excess cases of sleep disorders (95% CI, 19.4 to 27.6), 18.7 excess cases of anxiety (95% CI, 13.9 to 23.5), and 16.4 excess cases of acute stress reaction and adjustment disorders (95% CI, 12.2 to 20.6) (Alyssa, Jay, Stephen, Bradley, Joseph, Charles, & Engel, 2010).

The existing body of research related to growth and recovery from trauma and then propose an empirically informed and contextually sensitive model to guide future research with combat veterans. We draw from research focused on resilience, posttraumatic growth, and decline (negative or pathological) change trajectories, and we propose that meaning-making coping is a core mechanism of the posttraumatic growth process for combat veterans. Implications for practitioners and the next steps for future research are presented (Larner & Blow, 2011). A study was conducted by Herzog, Everson, and Whitworth (2011) in order to know the secondary trauma symptoms in spouse of combat-exposed National Guard soldiers mediate impact of social trauma exposure on their children. Result suggests that immediate family member of combat exposed soldiers with high level of were at risk of developing secondary traumatic stress. Secondary trauma symptom in the spouse was risk increasing mediating variable between trauma symptom in combat exposed soldiers and secondary trauma symptoms in children. Reports that long periods of overseas deployment in the armed forces are causes of stress, alcoholism, and other domestic problems appeared on the BBC and in several daily newspapers. The news reports were based on research that found that soldiers deployed for more than 13 months over a three-year period were more likely to "turn to drink, suffer post-traumatic stress disorder and have family rows" (Daily Express). The Daily Mail included the statistics that these troops were 58% more likely to develop post-traumatic stress disorder (PTSD) and "face a 35 % greater chance of becoming alcoholics". Descriptive evidence suggests that deployment in the Global war on Terrorism is associated with adverse mental Health; the causal effect of combat is not well established. Using data drawn from the National Longitudinal study of Adolescent Health, Rescul, Joseph and Erdal (2011) exploit exogenous variation in deployment assignment and find that soldiers deployed to combat zones where they engage in frequent enemy firefight or witness allied or civilian deaths are at substantially increased risk for suicidal ideation. Psychological counseling and Post-Traumatic Stress Disorder (PTSD). Our estimates imply lower-bound Health care costs of 1.5 to 2.7 billion for combat-induced PTSD. Such disorder is caused by the social factors.

The society enters into the life of the individual and makes him socially sick. Therefore, the social connection of the person either are associated with psychological distress or can be linked with psychological resilience especially depends on the resources the individual receives from his neighbourhood.

SOCIAL CONNECTEDNESS AND WELLBEING

Drinking practices vary substantially among different countries. An understanding of such differences can help researchers, clinicians, and policymakers develop prevention, diagnostic, and treatment measures as well as overall alcohol policies that are appropriate for a given country. Accordingly, researchers have conducted cross-cultural analyses of drinking patterns and practices. Three countries included in such analyses are India, Mexico, and Nigeria. These countries differ substantially in their ethnic and cultural characteristics, including the role that alcohol plays in daily life. To gain a better insight into the attitudes toward alcohol in these countries, researchers have analyzed the alcoholic beverage preferences, gender and age differences in alcohol consumption patterns, drinking contexts and drinking patterns, alcohol-related problems, approaches to prevention and treatment, and drinking indicators in each nation. These analyses demonstrate that no single definition of "normal" drinking, problem drinking, or alcohol dependence can apply equally to all countries or cultures (Bennett, Campillo, Chandrashekar, & Gureje, 1998). Economic context is a function of societal and communal economies. Developmental context deals with stages in life cycle (McGoldrick, 1999). Married service members are 2/3rd of total force and women only comprises of 14% in America (MFRC, 2000). The family's external context comprised of history, economics, and deployment of culture. The external context of family is usually outside the control of the family and affect the family's perception of military separation therefore influence stress (Boss, 2002). Such factor ranges from external to internal contexts. Families' historical context of past family stress influence family management of stress (Cozolino, 2002). Families' cultural context can provide valuable information for appropriate intervention. Families internal context consists of three factors: families structure (role), its psychology (Problem solving), and philosophy (belief).

There are few studies examining the relationship between psychopathology and positive experiences and traits. Although initial studies suggest persons with posttraumatic stress disorder (PTSD) are at increased risk for excessive social anxiety, there have been no studies to date evaluating how these conditions might interact to affect positive experiences and traits. Controlling for PTSD and trait negative affect, social anxiety was negatively related to global ratings of well-being and character strengths. Social anxiety also accounted for incremental variance in day-to-day well-being over a 14-day assessment period. Although veterans with PTSD reported lower levels of global and daily well-being and character strengths than veterans without PTSD, a diagnosis of PTSD failed to exhibit unique relationships with these constructs. Building on a growing body of work, these data suggest that social anxiety is uniquely associated with disturbances in positive experiences, events, and traits (Todd, Terri, Keith, & Gitendra, 2006).

The purpose of Eric , M., Flake, B.E. D., Patti, L. J., Laura S. (2009) study was to describe the psychosocial profile of school age children during parental deployment utilizing standardized psychosocial health and stress measures, and to identify predictors of children at "high risk" for psychosocial morbidity during wartime deployment.: Army spouses with a deployed service member and a child aged 5-12 years completed a deployment packet consisting of demographic and psychosocial questions. The psychosocial health measures included the Pediatric Symptom Checklist

(PSC), the Parenting Stress Index-Short Form and the Perceived Stress Scale-4. Results: Overall, 32% of respondents exceeded the PSC cut off score for their child, indicating "high risk" for psychosocial morbidity and 42% reported "high risk" stress on the Parenting Stress Index-Short Form. Parenting stress significantly predicted an increase in child psychosocial morbidity (odds ratio 7.41, confidence interval 2.9 -19.0, $p < 0.01$). Parents utilizing military support reported less child psychosocial morbidity (odds ratio 0.32, confidence interval 0.13- 0.77, $p < 0.01$) and parental college education was related to a decrease in child psychosocial morbidity (odds ratio 0.33, confidence interval 0.13- 0.81, $p < 0.02$). The effects of military rank, child gender, child age, and race or ethnic background did not reach statistical significance. The families in this study experiencing deployment identified one-third of military children at "high risk" for psychosocial morbidity. The most significant predictor of child psychosocial functioning during wartime deployment was parenting stress. Military, family and community supports help mitigate family stress during periods of deployment (Eric, Flake, Patti, & Laura S. 2009). Therefore, the well-being and quality of life can be understood and supported in the distinct arenas in which we live, work and interact.

Increasing stress on military family during war time is difficult for adolescent. A study was conducted by Mmari, Bradshaw, & Sudhinaraset (2010) on 11 focal military youth groups. Revealed that military youths are more worried about making frequent move. The parents and youths who have better social connectedness are well adjusted compared to their counterpart. Exposed a total of 56 naval enlisted males to laboratory conditions of isolation and confinement for 21 days. Variables included group size (dyads vs. triads), compatible vs. incompatible groups, crowding vs. less crowding (as measured by cu. ft/man), and junior vs. senior leadership. Ss then completed the Subjective Stress Scale and State-Trait Anxiety Inventory. Analysis indicates that Ss reported (a) higher subjective stress and state anxiety during isolation than during pre- and post isolation base-line periods, (b) greater hostility in junior-led and in incompatible groups, (c) a greater effect of crowding on subjective stress and state anxiety in triads, (d) greater hostility in less crowded rooms, (e) greater annoyance with physical aspects of the situation in compatible groups and in dyads, (f) greater anxiety in dyads, and (g) better adaptation to confinement in triads and in less crowded rooms. Results reflect the highly interactive nature of the relationships between the subjective reactions of individuals in groups and both social and physical aspects of the group setting. It is integrally linked to the vitality and abundance of natural resources relied upon for subsistence and cultural practices (Alexander, 2011).

MILITARY POLICIES OF INDIA AND WELLBEING

National security is the requirement to maintain the survival of the state through the use of economic, power projection and political power and the exercise of diplomacy. The concept developed mostly in the United States of America after World War II. Initially focusing on military might, it now encompasses a broad range of facets, all of which impinge on the non military or economic security of the nation and the values espoused by the national society. Accordingly, in order to possess national security, a nation needs to possess economic security, energy security, environmental security, etc. Security threats involve not only conventional foes such as other nation-states but also non-state actors such as violent non-state actors, narcotic cartels, multinational corporations and non-governmental organizations; some authorities include natural disasters and events causing severe environmental damage in this category. Measures taken to ensure national security include: using diplomacy to rally allies and isolate threats, marshalling economic power to facilitate or compel cooperation, maintaining effective armed forces, implementing civil defense and emergency preparedness measures (including anti-terrorism legislation), ensuring the resilience and redundancy of critical infrastructure, using intelligence services to detect and defeat or avoid threats and espionage, and to protect classified information, Using counterintelligence services or secret police to protect the nation from internal threats

The origin of the modern concept of "national security" as a philosophy of maintaining a stable nation state can be traced to the Peace of Westphalia, wherein the concept of a sovereign state, ruled by a sovereign, became the basis of a new international order of nation states.[8]:19 It was Thomas Hobbes in his 1651 work "Leviathan" who stated that citizens yield to a powerful sovereign who in turn promises an end to civil and religious war, and to bring forth a lasting peace, and give him the right to conduct policy, including wage war or negotiate for peace for the good of the "commonwealth", i.e. a mandate for national security. The Clausewitzian view of diplomacy and war being the instru-

ments of furthering national cause, added to the view of national security being sought by nations by exercising self-interest at all times (Haftendorn, 1991). This view came to be known as "classical realism" in international relations. Immanuel Kant, in his 1795 essay, "Perpetual Peace: A Philosophical Sketch" (Zum ewigen Frieden. Ein philosophischer Entwurf.), proposed a system where nation-states and dominating national interests were replaced by an enlightened world order, a community of mankind where nation-states subsumed the national interests under the rule of the international law because of rational insight, common good and moral commitment. National security was achieved by this voluntary accession by the leadership to a higher order than the nation-state, viz. "international security". Thus was born the "idealism" school of international relations.

In the last decades, the study of social policy and the literary production in this field has grown massively around the world. Naturally, this growing body of knowledge has contributed to identify different perspectives, or models, on the different role of government in social welfare. These normative perspectives-as they are frequently referred to-tend to be classified into two categories: the residual social policy model and the institutional social policy model. This biform has usually tended to be associated with Western European countries' social welfare (institutional approach) and United States (residual approach). However, in the 1980s, some scholars have argued that this dualism could not explain different social welfare experiences from other continents. In order to overcome this limitedness Midgley has coined the term social development or the developmental model of social policy. In this paper, the author traces the history of the developmental social policy perspective, describing its key theoretical premises and showing how it can be applied in practice (James, 2006). Numerous peace initiatives have been launched across the world. Vast amounts of resources have been utilized to craft peace agreements which have often collapsed under the weight of competing interests. It is necessary to examine whether there are other peace building strategies that can be adopted to complement existing efforts to promote peace on the continent.

The study of Murithi (2006) examines African indigenous approaches to building peace and promoting social solidarity. It will begin by looking at the reasons why it is necessary to build peace. The paper will then look at the role that indigenous approaches are playing in promoting peace. It will also examine how these approaches emphasize the importance of promoting social solidarity. To enable culture to begin to play a significant role in the reconstruction of Africa, it will be necessary to establish education and training programs based on progressive African cultural values for officials, civil society actors and citizens - keeping in mind that not all traditions are empowering, particularly on issues with regard to gender equality. Progressive cultural principles which promote human dignity and the well-being of the individual and society can provide valuable insights into how Africa can be peacefully reconstructed by using its own indigenous value-systems which emphasize promoting social solidarity. Promoting social solidarity in practice means confronting corruption and trying to ensure democratic governance, power sharing, and the equitable distribution of resources among all members of the society. The study concludes by examining the strategies that can be adopted for increasing the use of indigenous approaches to building peace and social solidarity in Africa. Central upon New Delhi, contemporary India's strategic culture mainly meant Nehruvian that is Jawarlal Nehru's views about security and the world, in a rather long time. Later on, with the weakening of the dominance of Nehruvian, India's strategic culture experienced constant changes. India's nuclear strategy is closely associated with its strategic culture in the following three ways: (1) In a rather long period of time, due to the restriction of Nehruvian, India had been slow on the path of nuclear- weaponization ; (2) The weakening of the dominant role of Nehruvian is the prerequisite of India's nuclear- weaponization ; (3) The new strategic concept represented by the strategic elites of the Bhartiya Janta Party (BJP) is the crucial reason of India's open nuclear deterrence (Jiegen, 2007). The European Union has developed its security competence since 1992, thus putting pressure on its Member States to provide troops for the increasing number of EU peace operations being deployed to different areas of the globe. But with national militaries being rationalized and contracted the EU will inevitably follow the lead of the US, the UK, and the UN and start to use Private Military Contractors to undertake some of the functions of peace operations (EJIL, 2008).

As an academic concept, national security can be seen as a recent phenomenon which was first introduced in the United States after World War II, and has to some degree replaced other concepts that describe the struggle of states to overcome various external and internal threats. The earliest mention of the term national security, however, was made in Yale University in 1790 wherein reference was made to its relation with domestic industries (Paleri, 2008). The concept of national security became an official guiding principle of foreign policy in the United States when the National Security Act of 1947 was signed on July 26, 1947 by U.S. President Harry S. Truman. Together with its 1949 amendment, this act created important facets for American national security such as the precursor to the Department of Defense), subordinated the military branches to the new cabinet level position of the Secretary of Defense, established the National Security Council and the Central Intelligence Agency(Davis, 2010). The Act did not define national security which was conceivably advantageous as it's ambiguity made it a powerful phrase to invoke whenever issues threatened by other interests of the state, such as domestic concerns, came up for discussion and decision.

The realization that national security encompasses more than just military security was present, though understated, from the beginning itself. The US National Security Act of 1947 was set up "to advise the President on the integration of domestic, military and foreign policies relating to national security". Gen. Maxwell Taylor's essay of 1974 titled "The Legitimate Claims of National Security" has this to say: The national valuables in this broad sense include current assets and national interests, as well as the sources of strength upon which our future as a nation depends. Some valuables are tangible and earthy; others are spiritual or intellectual. They range widely from political assets such as the Bill of Rights, our political institutions and international friendships, to many economic assets which radiate worldwide from a highly productive domestic economy supported by rich natural resources. It is the urgent need to protect valuables such as these which legitimizes and makes essential the role of national security.

Soft powers importance has increased in the context of globalization and the growing disquiet over the use of military power for achieving foreign policy objectives. This paper focuses specifically on soft power in India's foreign policy and sources of India's soft power inimically and how to increase its soft power(Purushothaman, 2010). Information technology systems have transformed the citizen into a global participant-observer (GPO). The emerging GPO is innovative in networking, observation, and participation through autonomous, reflective, informative, inquisitive and self-organizing means of engagement. Classic citizenship is an ingredient of the nation-state. With globalization and the increased interconnectedness among people of various countries through the use of information and communication technology (ICT), the new citizen of the world is transcending traditional cultural, economic, and political barriers to demand openness, accountability, and fairness. This article contrasts between the classic citizen of the nation-state and the emerging GPO. It then outlines the characteristics of the new global participant-observers and the phenomenon's Strengths, weaknesses, opportunities, and threats (Alexander, 2011).

INTERVENTIONS AND PSYCHOLOGICAL WELL-BEING

The goal of the current policy is one of zero tolerance toward drug and alcohol abuse. Programmatic areas to help attain this goal are assessment, deterrence and detection, treatment and rehabilitation, and education and training. Progress toward eliminating drug and alcohol abuse among military personnel is traced by examining efforts in each of these programmatic areas. Result reported dramatic decreases in drug use and more stable patterns of alcohol use since 1980 indicate that military efforts to eliminate alcohol abuse should be intensified (Robert & Mary, 1992). Cannon-Bowers, Salas, Tannenbaumscott, & Mathew (1995) Investigated a model of training effectiveness to define the impact of individual factors that trainees bring to the training environment, and their ability to acquire and apply targeted skills. Navy recruits completed attitude, self- efficacy and training motivation scales. Results indicate that several non-technical trainee related factors had a significant impact on training outcome; self-efficacy, task related attitudes, expectations for training, training fulfillment and pertaining motivation.

The article of Ballone 2000 focuses on the role and development of military psychology in the South African context. Peacekeeping operations and the results of the first and fifth deployment of the South African National Defense Force (SANDF) in the Democratic Republic of Congo (DRC) are used as background to illustrate the relevance of military psychology in such operations. Peacekeeping operations involve military and often civilian personnel. The nature of peacekeeping operations has become increasingly complex and stressful. It is hypothesized that the stressors that members experience may have a destructive effect on their morale and on the cohesion of the force, and that it could lead to alcohol and drug abuse. Teaching mental skills for self-esteem enhancement in a military healthcare setting by the need exists for educational methods which can positively influence self-esteem, especially in demanding military health care settings. Warrior Transition units (WTU's) are tasked with the challenging mission of caring for seriously injured or ill U.S Army soldiers. This paper explored the hypothesis that an educationally-based mental skills Training (MST) intervention can enhance self-esteem in members of a warrior Transition unit in the U.S Army. The sample was comprised of 27 WTU cadre members who participated in an Army center for Enhanced Performance (ACEP) MST educational workshop at a large Army installation on the west coast. Instruments included the Ottawa Mental Skills Inventory (OMSAT-3; Durand-Bush & Salmela, 2001) and the self-esteem Rating scale (SERS; Wagnild, 1993). Results showed that SERS scores were significantly higher following the intervention. Furthermore, the ACEP instructional components of self. Confidence, imagery and mental practice were significant predictors of self-esteem. Results suggest that MST might be a viable educational approach for enhancing self-esteem in the WTU cadre (Hammermeister, Michael & Carl, 2009).

Stress associated with overseas military service is a major concern for soldiers, their families, and communities whereas actual deployment is the most obvious disruption, pre-

deployment (preparing to go overseas) and post-deployment (re-integration into family and community) also cause significant stress. Several authors have suggested that when considering interventions to ease military service related stress, it is critical to take into account not only the individual as a "client" but also how military families are embedded in larger communities, and how interventions can build on existing informal and social networks and other community assets. Although largely absent from the research literature focusing on individual therapy and on community capacity in military communities, individual veterans, conservation organizations, and government agencies across the US and in the UK are initiating projects that connect returning soldiers to nature, through gardening, farming, job skills, hunting, fishing, retreat centers, camps, and outdoor adventure experiences. These initiatives are perhaps not surprising, given that extensive research from the fields of horticultural therapy and conservation psychology has demonstrated the positive outcomes of contact with nature for individual and community well-being and healing (Tidball, & Marianne, 2010).

The objective of Parkkari, et al. (2011)' study was to investigate whether a neuromuscular training program with injury prevention counseling is effective in preventing acute musculoskeletal injuries in young men during military service. Two successive cohorts of male conscripts in four companies of one brigade in the Finnish Defense Forces were first followed prospectively for one 6-month term to determine the baseline incidence of injury. After this period, two new successive cohorts in the same four companies were randomized into two groups and followed prospectively for 6 months. Military service is compulsory for about 90% of 19-year-old Finnish men annually, who comprised the cohort in this study. This randomized, controlled trial included 968 conscripts comprising 501 conscripts in the intervention group and 467 conscripts in the control group. A neuromuscular training program was used to enhance conscripts' motor skills and body control, and an educational injury prevention program was used to increase knowledge and awareness of acute musculoskeletal injuries. The main outcome measures were acute injuries of the lower and upper limbs. Results revealed that in the intervention groups, the risk for acute ankle injury decreased significantly compared to control groups (adjusted hazards ratio (HR) = 0.34, 95% confidence interval (95% CI) = 0.15 to 0.78, P = 0.011). This risk decline was observed in conscripts with low as well as moderate to high baseline fitness levels. In the latter group of conscripts, the risk of upper-extremity injuries also decreased significantly (adjusted HR = 0.37, 95% CI 0.14 to 0.99, P = 0.047). In addition, the intervention groups tended to have less time loss due to injuries (adjusted HR = 0.55, 95% CI 0.29 to 1.04). A neuromuscular training and injury prevention counseling programme was effective in preventing acute ankle and upper-extremity injuries in young male army conscripts.

Resilience has been regarded narrowly as a quintessential individual property by most investigators. Social resilience, however, is inherently a multilevel construct, revealed by capacities of individuals, but also groups, to foster, engage in, and sustain positive social relationships and to endure and recover from stressors and social isolation. Emergent levels of organization, ranging from dyads, families, and groups to cities, civilizations, and international alliances have long been apparent in human existence, but identifying the features of individuals, relationships, and group structures and norms that promote social resilience-and determining effective interventions to build social resilience-represent some of the most important challenges facing the military as well as contemporary behavioral science. We identify nine personal resources that foster social resilience, and we describe an educational, computer-based program that builds on these resources in an effort to improve the social resilience among troops in the U.S. Army (John, Harry, & Alex, 2011).

The military personnel therefore are prone to various types of stressors compared to their counterpart civilian. They do have to follow the norm of the military that is highly stressful. On the one hand the national security is their top priority on the other hand they are also the common men who have their own family, spouse, children, friends and neighbourhood. The married life further exerts their influence on their work performance. The deployment cycle further aggravate their suffering. Nomadic nature of military life makes them prone to psychological and physical stressor. For example the military personnel of rural and hilly areas are unable to bear the heat. Similarly the personnel belonging to plain areas are unable to bear the wave of the cold. Therefore, it becomes necessary to study their wellbeing that involves positive and negative indicators. The positive indicators depict e.g. life satisfaction, happiness, self-esteem and self-efficacy whereas the negative indicators deal with anxiety, depression, suicidal thoughts, as well as substances uses. Therefore the present study intends to hypothesize the same between civilian and military personnel. The detailed hypotheses are as under:-

HYPOTHESES

1. *There will be a significance difference between military personnel and civilians on the dimensions of psychological wellbeing (Life satisfaction, wellbeing, self-esteem, depression, alcohol, smoking and substance uses).*
2. *There will be a significance difference between married and unmarried military personnel and civilians on various dimension of psychological wellbeing (Life satisfaction, wellbeing, self-esteem, depression, alcohol, smoking and substance uses).*
3. *There will be a significance difference between Himachali and Non-Himachali married and unmarried military personnel and civilians on various dimension of psychological wellbeing (Life satisfaction, wellbeing, self-esteem, depression, alcohol, smoking and substance uses).*

CHAPTER 4

METHODOLOGY

The objective of the Present Study is to identify the difference between military personnel and civilians on various dimension of psychological wellbeing (Life satisfaction, wellbeing, self-esteem, depression, alcohol, smoking and substance uses). Further the objective is to make out the difference between married and unmarried military personnel and civilians on various dimension of psychological wellbeing (Life satisfaction, wellbeing, self-esteem, depression, alcohol, smoking and substance uses). Finally the study also intends to identify the difference between Himachali and Non-Himachali married and unmarried military personnel and civilians on various dimension of psychological wellbeing (Life satisfaction, wellbeing, self-esteem, depression, alcohol, smoking and substance uses). For attaining the objective the study has been conducted on Subathu Military Cantonment that is located in District Solan of Himachal Pradesh (India). The description of study area is as follows:-

STUDY AREA

The study was conducted in Subathu area of district Solan which is located on National highway-22 situated in Himachal Pradesh (India). The study has been conducted in Army area of Subathu which is known as 14 Gorkha Training Center (14.G.T.C). From here, the nearest railway station is Dharampur which is just 15 kilometers. The Subathu is approximately 60 kilometers from the Shimla and Chandigarh. It is approachable through public and private transport. The appropriate study site (map) has been shown in the below mentioned figure.

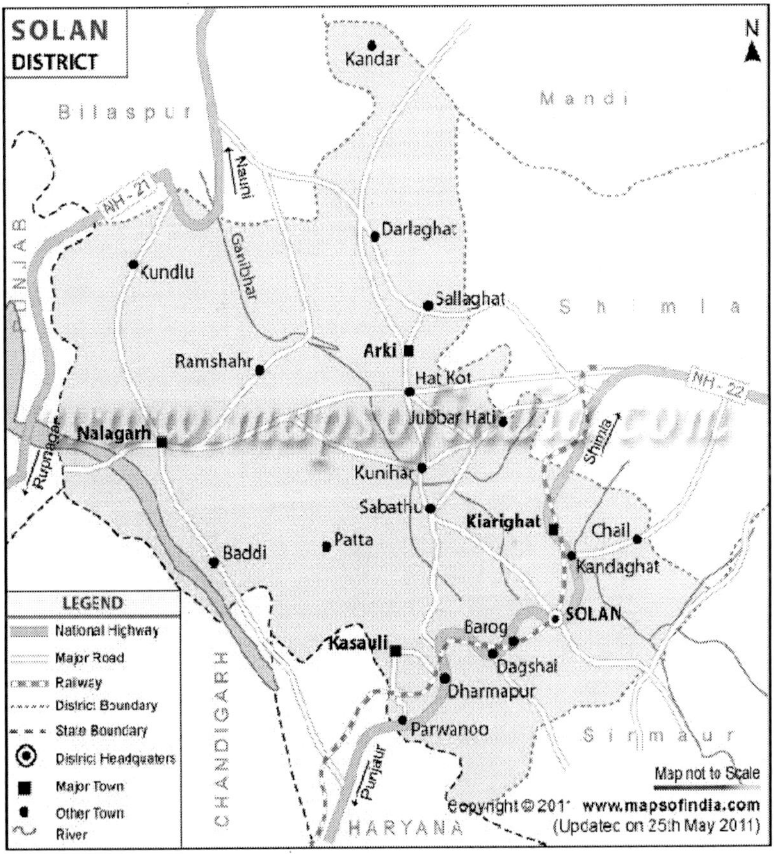

Fig. 4.1: Map of District Solan

Fig. 4.2: Showing map of Subathu Cantonment Area of District Solan H.P.

SAMPLE CLASSIFICATION

In the present study a sample of N=120 subjects has been selected from the Subathu of the district Solan. The sample selected in the present study was from 25-40 year of age. The selected sample of N=120 subjects were divided into two sub-groups based on their profession i.e. from Military (N=60) and from civil (N=60) subjects. These subjects were again divided into two equal comparable half based on their marital status that comprises of N=30 married as well as another N=30 unmarried. Finally, the subjects were again sub-divided into two comparable halves based on their Domicile that comprises of N=15 Himachali and remaining N=15 Non-Himachali. In all, there were eight groups with N=15 subjects in each that comprise of complete sample of 120 subjects of aforesaid characteristics. Sample classification is as follows

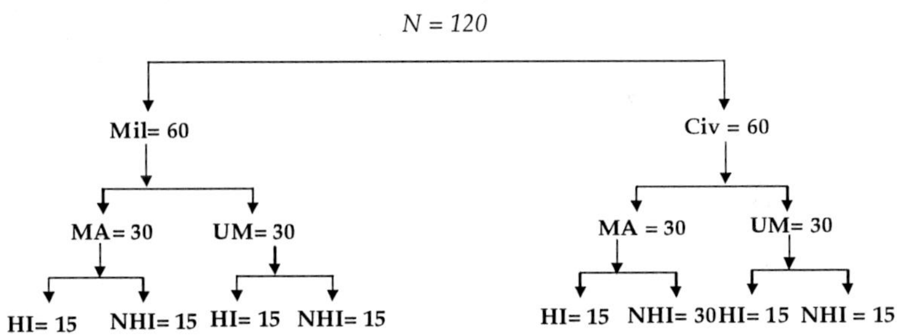

Notations: Mil= Military; Civ. = Civilian; MA= Married; UM = Unmarried; HI=Himachali; NHI=Non-Himachali

Fig. 4.3: Sample classification

MEASURES

In this study both quantitative and qualitative measures have been used. The description is as follows

Life Satisfaction Scale

This scale was developed by Ramji Shrivastava' in 1971. It consists of 60 items related to six areas viz, health, personal, economic, marital, social, and job. The responses are to be given in yes/no form. The yes responses indicate the satisfaction those in this scale is assigned one (1) mark whereas No responses is weighted with zero (0) marks. The sum of marks is obtained for the entire scale. Higher the score more will be the life satisfaction. The scales generally take 20 minutes to complete. This scale has r =.84 e test retest reliability and the validity quotient ranges from r = 74 to r = .82 respectively. The maximum score of the scale is 60.

P.G.I General Well-Being Measure

The PGI general well-being measure developed by Verma and Verma (1989) in Hindi version consists of 20 items those are related to subjective feelings of contentment, happiness, satisfaction, and sense of achievement. It generally took five to ten minutes to complete and can be administered on all age including to the illiterate people as well. The score ranges from 0 to 20. Higher the score greater will the general wellbeing. The reliability of Hindi version measure is r = .86.

State Self-Esteem Scale

It was developed by Heatherton and Polivy in 1991. It has 20 items in all. It is a five point scale. The items No. 2, 4, 5, 7, 8, 10, 13, 15, 16, 17, 18, 19 and 20 follow reverse scoring. The score ranges from minimum of 20 to the maximum of 100. Higher the score greater will be the self-esteem. The reliability of the scale ranges from r = 0.73 to r = –0.81. The SSES appears to be a useful measure for assessing state self-esteem in stroke patients.

Alcohol, Smoking and Substance Involvement Screening Test (ASSIST)

This test was developed by the 'World Health Organization' (WHO) in 2001. It contains 8 items those are related to different situations. It is a brief screening questionnaire used to find out people's involvement in Alcohol, smoking and substances. Each question on the ASSIST has a set of responses. Item No. one has only two options in the form of Yes and No whereas items No.2 to 6 has five options and remaining two items i.e. item No. 7 and 8 have four options. Thus, the score ranges from 0 to 25. Higher the score more vulnerable the person will be in ASSIST. The Average test-retest reliability coefficient's ranges from a high of 0.90 to 0.58.

Beck Depression Inventory

The Beck Depression Inventory developed by Dr. Aaron Beck in 1961 contains 21-multiple choice questions that are most widely used for measuring the severity of depression. It is a four point scale where the score ranges from minimum of zero to the maximum of 21. Higher score represent more depression. It is a reliable and valid tool used across the world.

Observation

Observation is a fundamental aspect of any science and has been playing an essential part in the development of psychology as a scientific discipline. Observation involves the noting and recording of events and human behavior without formal manipulation of variables operating in the events.

Interview

Interview is a formal or informal meeting between two or among a group of people for the purpose of obtaining information about something in particular. It is face to face conversation which is always goal directed. It is considered as a successful tool in social sciences research.

Fuzzy Cognitive Mapping (FCM)

Individuals store their own perception of the reality through mental maps. In cognitive maps, the stored concepts are decoded, analyzed and clearly structured through cause and effect relationships, and this is significantly useful both for individual aims (through understanding of complex issues) and in group situations. A cognitive map is constituted by nodes, which represents the concepts and are connected to each other by links (also called edges). The edges are directed to show the directions of the cause-effect relationships. The fuzzy cognitive maps Developed initially by Kosllo in 1986 and later by Ozesmi in 1999 and 2006 deals with explore cognitive maps of the individual and groups.

Photography

Photography is the process of forming stable or permanent visible directly or indirectly by the action of light or other forms of radiation on sensitive surfaces.

PROCEDURE

Subathu is located on the foothills of the Himalayas and is 20 kilometers from Solan. It is still considered as a cantonment area and is popular as the Regimental Center of the Gorkha Rifles, which depict the chivalry and courage of the warriors. The objective of the present study is to study is to compare the Military personnel and Civilian on the dimensions of psychological wellbeing. More appropriately the objective of the study is to identify the difference between military personnel and civilians on various dimension of psychological wellbeing (Life satisfaction, wellbeing, self-esteem, depression, alcohol, smoking and substance uses). Further the study also intends to identify the difference between married and unmarried military personnel and civilians on various dimension of psychological wellbeing (Life satisfaction, wellbeing, self-esteem, depression, alcohol, smoking and substance uses). Similarly the study further makes out the difference between Himachali and Non-Himachali married and unmarried military personnel and civilians on various dimension of psychological wellbeing (Life satisfaction, wellbeing, self-esteem, depression, alcohol, smoking and substance uses). For accomplishing the objective the study has been conducted on a sample of N=120 those were divided into two sub-groups based on their profession i.e. from Military (N=60) and civil (N=60). These subjects were again sub-divided into two comparable half based on their marital status that comprises of N=30 married as well as another N=30 unmarried. Finally, the subjects were divided into two comparable half based on their domicile that comprises of N=15 Himachali as well as another N=15 non-Himachali. In all, there were eight groups with N=15 subjects in each that comprise of a complete sample of 120 subjects of aforesaid characteristics. These eight groups were assessed with the help of qualitative and quantitative measures. The qualitative measure include, field observation, interview, fuzzy cognitive mapping and photography whereas the quantitative measure include the life satisfaction scale, state self-esteem scale, Alcohol, smoking, substance involvement screening test, PGI General well-being measure and Beck's depression inventory. The quantitative measure is self-report in nature that was administered by the researcher herself by asking open ended question, from the participants. Since the researcher herself dealt with Subathu area of district Solan, therefore, it helped a lot in asking questions to the local dialects from the civilians while carrying out descriptive information. Beside this the researcher did her pilot study and asked various people about the problems in military. The researcher entered in the particular area, by establishing warmth atmospheres with the participants followed with addressing the goal.

The ideas elicited by the subjects were welcomed by the researcher and they were encouraged to explain more about the problems in military. The researcher used observation, interview, fuzzy cognitive mapping as well as photography to record the life of the army personnel. Though qualitative analysis their view were record and described in the result section. Beside this the subjects were analyzed though life satisfaction scale, state self-esteem scale, alcohol smoking substance involvement screening test, PGI General well-being measure and Beck's 'depression inventory in order to record qualitative data about the psycho-socio issues in military so as to verify the dependent variable justified and scientifically. Their scores were tabulated and means were compared and analyzed by performing three way analysis of variance. The description of the result has been presented in the next chapter.

CHAPTER 5

GENERAL WELLBEING AMONG MILITARY AND CIVILIAN

We must have unification in organization, armaments, training, discipline and other fields, for the high degree of centralization of command needed in modern warfare so as to advance the modernization of army. Every member of our army must strictly obey orders, self-consciously observe discipline, promote the sense of accuracy, planning and organization and oppose individualism (Su Yu, 1954)

QUANTITATIVE ANALYSIS

Life Satisfaction among the Military and Civilians

Life satisfaction represents how satisfied people feel with their life generally, as contrasted with positive affect, which represents how they feel at a single point in time. That is, life satisfaction involves people thinking about their life as a whole, including factors such as whether they are achieving their goals. These five traits will find more life satisfaction; gratitude, ability to love and be loved, curiosity, zest for life and spirituality.

Table 5.1

A 2 X 2 X 2 ANOVA Performed on Himachali and on-Himachali Married and Unmarried Military and Civilian People on Life Satisfaction Scale

Source	SS	df	ms	F	P
Total	192249.000	120			
P	195.075	1	195.075	6.61	.01
M	2125.208	1	2125.208	71.98	.001
D	170.408	1	170.408	5.77	.01
P x M	18.408	1	18.408	.623	n.s.
P x D	14.008	1	14.008	.474	n.s.
M x D	44.408	1	44.408	1.50	n.s.
P x M x D	12.675	1	12.675	.429	n.s.
Error	3306.800	112	29.525		

Notations: P = Profession; M = Marital status; D = Domicile

From the Table 5.1, it is quite clear that the main effect of profession on the measure of life satisfaction was found F (1,112) = 6.61, p<.01 as statistically significant. The military people were found more satisfied from their counterpart. Therefore hypothesis No. 1 which states that "There will be *a significance difference between military personnel and civilians on the dimensions of psychological wellbeing" is accepted.*

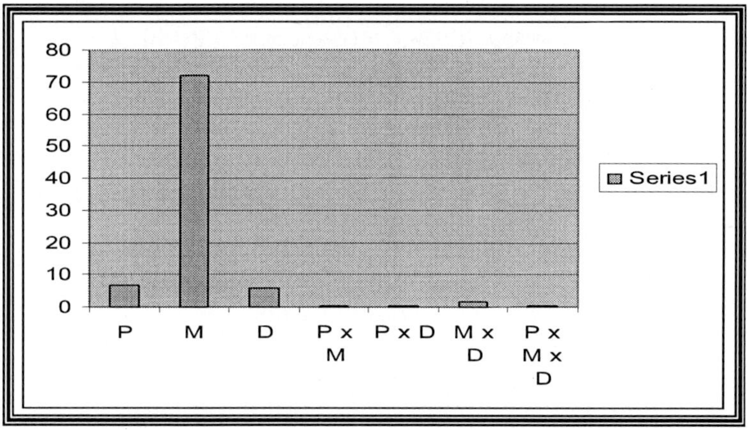

Fig. 5.1 Showing F values among Himachali and non-Himachali married and unmarried military personnel and civilian on life satisfaction.

Similarly, the main effect of marital status was also found F (1,112) = 71.98, 0<.001 as highly significant. The married people were found more satisfied from their life compared to their counterpart. Therefore hypothesis No. 2 which states that "There will be a significance difference between married and unmarried military personnel and civilians on various dimension of psychological wellbeing" is accepted. Further the main effect of domicile was found F (1,112) = 5.77, p < .01 as statistically significant. Himachali personnel were found more satisfied from their life as compared to their counterpart. Therefore hypothesis No. 3 which states that "There will be a significance difference between Himachali and Non-Himachali married and unmarried military personnel and civilians on various dimension of *psychological wellbeing " is accepted. The F value is as follows:-*

It shows that all the above three factors have played significant role in the dependent measure i.e. Life Satisfaction. Further two way interaction between Px M was found F (1,112) = .62, p>.05 as statistically non-significant. Similarly the two way interaction between P x D was found F (1, 112) = .47, p>.05 as non significant. Further two way interaction between M x D was also found F (1,112) = 1.50, p>.05 as non significant. Finally three way interaction between M x D x P was found F (1,112) = .42, p>.05 as non significant. It shows that the two ways and three way interaction of the aforesaid variable have not contributed a lot in the measure of life Satisfaction.

SELF-ESTEEM AMONG MILITARY AND CIVILIAN

Self-esteem is a term in Psychology to reflect a person's overall evaluation or appraisal of his or her own worth. Self-esteem encompasses beliefs and emotions such as triumph, despair, pride and shame. Self-esteem include: self-worth, self-regard, self-respect and self-integrity. Self-esteem as automatic and inevitable consequences of the sum of individuals' choices in using their consciousness.

From the Table 5.2, it is quite clear that the main effect of profession on the measure of self-esteem was found F (1,112) = 4.41, p<.05 as statistically significant. Military people reported more self-esteem compared to their counterpart. Therefore hypothesis No. 1 which states that "There will be a significance difference between military personnel and civilians on the dimensions of psychological wellbeing" is accepted. Similarly *the main effect marital status was also found F (1,112) = .13, p>.05 as statistically non significant. Married people reported more self-esteem than to comparison group. Therefore hypothesis NO 2 which states that "There will be a significance difference between married and unmarried military personnel and civilians on various dimension of psychological wellbeing" is accepted.*

Table 5.2

A 2 X 2 X 2 ANOVA Performed on Himachali and non-Himachali Married and Unmarried Military and Civilian People on Self-esteem

Source	SS	df	ms	F	P
Total	706637.000	120			
P	371.008	1	371.008	4.41	.05
M	11.408	1	11.408	.13	n. s.
D	138.675	1	138.675	1.65	n. s.
P x M	541.875	1	541.875	6.44	.01
P x D	33.075	1	33.075	.39	n. s.
M x D	78.408	1	78.408	.93	n. s.
P x M x D	21.675	1	21.675	.26	n. s.
Error	9429.867	112	84.195		

Notations: P = Profession; M = Marital status; D = Domicile

Further the main effect of Domicile was found F (1,112) = 1.64, p>.05 as statistically non significant. It shows that all the above three factors have not played significant role in the dependent measure i.e. state self esteem. Further two way interaction between P x M was found F (1,112) = 6.44, p<.01, as statistically significant. Similarly the two way interaction between P x D was found F (1,112) = .39, p, p>.05 as statistically non significant. The F-values have also been plotted in the below mentioned figure.

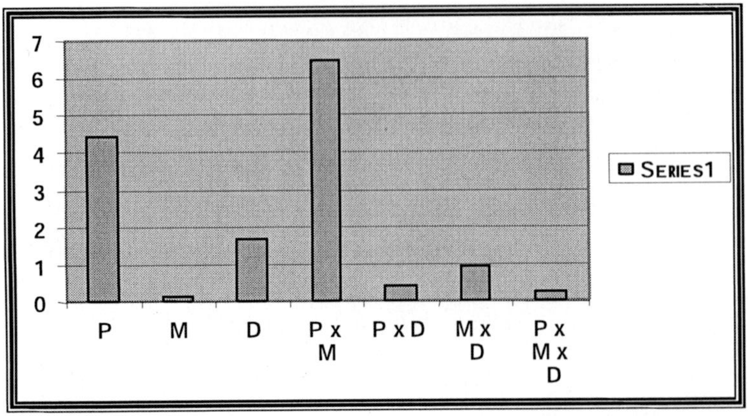

Fig. 5.2 Showing F values among Himachali and Non-Himachali married and unmarried military personnel and civilian on self-esteem

Further, the two way interaction between M x D was found F (1,112) = .93, p >.05 as statistically non significant. Finally, the three way interaction between M x D x P was F (1,112) = .25, p >.05 as statistically non significant. It shows that the two ways and three way interaction of the aforesaid variable have not contributed a lot in the measure of State Self- esteem.

ALCOHOL, SMOKING, SUBSTANCE INVOLVEMENT AMONG MILITARY AND CIVILIAN PEOPLE

Substance abuse, also known as drug abuse, refers to a maladaptive pattern of use of a substance that is not considered dependent. The term 'drug abuse' does not exclude dependency, but is otherwise used in a similar manner in non-medical contexts, use of these drugs may lead to criminal penalty in addition to possible physical, social and psychological harm, both strongly depending on local jurisdiction.

Table 5.3

A 2 X 2 X 2 ANOVA Performed on Himachali and non-Himachali Married and Unmarried Military and Civilian People on ASSIST

Source	SS	df	Ms	F	P
Total	5210.000	120			
P	.300	1	.300	.05	n. s.
M	24.300	1	24.300	1.33	n. s.
D	6.533	1	6.533	.35	n. s.
P x M	9.633	1	9.633	.52	n. s.
P x D	136.533	1	136.533	7.47	.01
M x D	3.333	1	3.333	.18	n. s.
P x M x D	3.333	1	3.333	.18	n. s.
Error	2046.000	112	18.268		

Notations: P = Profession; M = Marital status; D = Domicile

From the Table 5.3 it is quite clear that the main effect of profession in the measure of substance abuse was found F (1,112) = .016, p>.05 as statistically non significant. Very slight difference was found between the two groups. Therefore hypothesis No. 1 which states that "There will be a significance difference between military personnel and civilians on the dimensions of psychological wellbeing" is rejected.

Similarly the main effect of marital status was also found F (1,112) = 1.33, p >.05 as statistically non significant. Further the main effect of Domicile was found F (1,112) = .35, p>.05 as statistically non significant. Here again hypothesis No. 2 which states that "There will be a significance difference between married and unmarried military personnel and civilians on various dimension of psychological wellbeing" *is rejected. It shows that all the above three factors have not played significant role in the dependent measure i.e., Substance Abuse. Further two way interaction between P x M was found F (1,112) = .52, p>.05 as statistically non significant. Similarly the two way interaction between P x D was found F (1, 112) =7.47, p<.01 as statistically significant. Further, the two way interaction between M x D was found F (1,112) =.18 p >.05 as statistically non significant.*

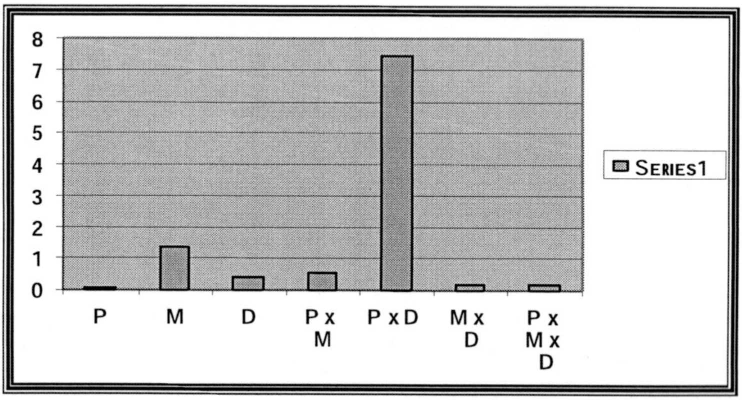

Fig. 5.3 Showing F values among Himachali Non-Himachali married and unmarried military personnel and civilian on ASSIST

Finally, the three way interaction between M x D x P was found F = 1,112 = .18, p>.05 as statistically non significant. It shows that the two way and three way interaction of the aforesaid variable have not contributed a lot in the measure of Substance Abuse.

GENERAL WELLBEING AMONG MILITARY AND CIVILIAN

The term quality of life is used to evaluate the general well-being of individuals and societies. The term is used in a wide range of contexts, including the fields of international developments, healthcare and politics. Quality of life should not be confused with the concept of standard of living, which is based primarily on income. Instead, standard indicators of the quality of include not only wealth and employment, physical and mental health, education, recreation and leisure time, and social belonging.

Table 5.4

A 2 X 2 X 2 ANOVA Performed on Himachali and on-Himachali Married and Unmarried Military and Civilian People on general well being

Source	SS	df	Ms	F	p
Total	35299.000	120			
P	114.075	1	114.075	20.30	.001
M	23.408	1	23.408	4.16	.05
D	10.208	1	10.208	1.81	n.s.
P x M	46.875	1	46.875	8.34	.01
P x D	5.208	1	5.208	.927	n.s.
M x D	9.075	1	9.075	1.61	n.s.
P x M x D	18.408	1	18.408	3.27	.05
Error	629.333	112	5.619		

Notations: P = Profession; M = Marital status; D = Domicile

From the table 5.4, it is quite clear that the main effect of profession was found F (1,112) = 20.30, p<.001 as statistically significant. The military people reported more wellbeing compared to their counterpart. Therefore, hypothesis No. 1 which states that "There will be a significance difference between military personnel and civilians on the dimensions of psychological wellbeing" is accepted.

Similarly the main effect of marital status was also found F (1,112) = 4.16, p<.05 as statistically significant. Married *people reported more wellbeing compared to comparison group. Therefore hypothesis No. 2 which states that "There will be a significance difference between married and unmarried military personnel and civilians on various dimension of psychological wellbeing" is accepted.*

Further the main effect of Domicile was found F (1,112) = 1.81, p>.05 as statistically non significant. It shows that two factors have played significant role in the dependent measure i.e. PGI General Well being. But it also shows that one factor have not played significant role in the dependent measure i.e. PGI General Well-being. Further two way interaction between P x M was found as F (1,112) = 8.34, p<.01 as statistically significant. Similarly two way interaction between P x D was found F (1,112) = .92, p >.05 as statistically non significant.

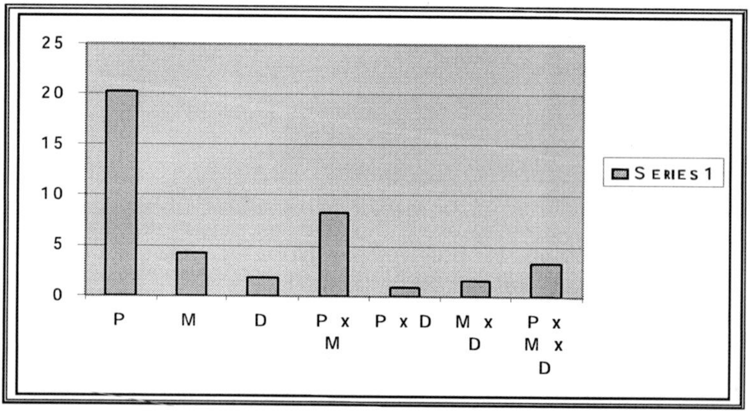

Fig 5.4 Showing F value in general well-being among military and civilian people

Further the two way interaction between M x D was found F (1,112) = 1.61, p>.05 as statistically non significant. Finally the three way interaction between M x D x P was *found F (1,112) = 3.27, p <.05 as statistically non significant. It shows that the two way ad three way interaction of the aforesaid variable have contributed little in the measure of PGI General Well-being.*

DEPRESSION AMONG MILITARY AND CIVILIAN PEOPLE

Depression is a state of low mood and aversion to activity that can affect a person's thoughts, behaviors, feelings and physical well-being. Depressed people may feel sad, anxious, empty, hopeless, helpless, worthless, guilty, irritable or restless. Depressed mood is a normal reaction to certain life events, a symptom of some medical conditions and treatments and a feature of certain psychiatric syndromes.

Table 5.5

A 2 X 2 X 2 ANOVA Performed on Himachali and on-Himachali Married and Unmarried Military and Civilian People on Beck's Depression Inventory

Source	SS	df	Ms	F	P
Total	27142.000	120			
P	760.033	1	760.033	13.03	.001
M	32.033	1	32.033	.54	n. s.
D	13.333	1	13.333	.23	n. s.
P x M	132.300	1	132.300	2.27	n. s.
P x D	529.200	1	529.200	9.07	.01
M x D	43.200	1	43.200	.74	n. s.
P x M x D	97.200	1	97.200	1.67	n. s.
Error	6533.867	112	58.338		

Notations: P = Profession; M = Marital status; D = Domicile

From the table 5.5, it is quite clear that the main effect of profession was found F (1,112) =13.03, p<.001 as statistically *significant. Civilian reported more depression compared to their counterpart. Therefore, hypothesis No. 1 which states that "There will be a significance difference between military personnel and civilians on the dimensions of psychological wellbeing" is accepted.*

Similarly, the main effect of Martial status was also found F (1,112) =.54, p >.05 as statistically non significant. Further the main effect of Domicile was found F (1,112) =.23, p >.05 as statistically non significant. It shows that one factor has plays significant role in the dependent measure i.e. Beck's Depression Inventory. But it also shows that the above two factors have not played any significant role in the dependence measures that is Beck's Depression inventory.

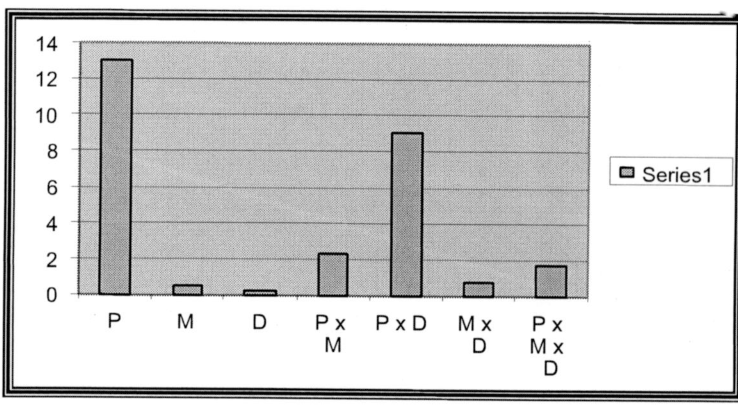

Fig. 5.5 Showing F values among Himachali Non-Himachali married and unmarried military personnel and civilian on Beck's Depression Inventory

Further two way interaction between P x M was found F (1,112) = 2.27, p >.05 as statistically non-significant. Similarly, the two way interaction between P x D was found F (1,112) = 9.07, p <.01 as statistically significant.

Further the two way interaction between M x D was found F (1,112) =.74, p >.05 as statistically non significant. Finally the three way interaction between M x D x P was found F (1,112) =1.67, p >.05 as statistically non significant. It shows that the two ways and three way interaction of the aforesaid variable have contributed very little in the measure of Beck's Depression Inventory.

QUALITATIVE FINDINGS

PHYSICAL PROBLEMS

During field study it was found that some military person suffered from blood pressure problem followed with cholesterol problem. Further obesity was observed among the soldiers. The reasons for these problems are due to less involvement in fitness programs and more inclination toward eating habit that involves saturated fats like meat, oil, ghee, milk, butter and cheese and more salt intake followed with use of pickle to and excessive spices in their food. Further, habit of consuming alcohol and other substances such as cigarette, tobaccos, pan-supari and gutka etc. further increase allostatic load on their physical health. Further the soldier has to bear different weather conditions that affect their health. The experience of civil war is also directly associated with their health hazards. The post war situation is related to cardiac, gastrointestinal, and other medical related problem throughout their lives. People who serve in the Military and veterans face some different health issues than civilians. During war time, the main health concerns are life threatening injuries. These include shrapnel and gunshot wounds, lost limbs, and head injuries. Some members reported that they are prone towards health problems resulting from environmental hazards, such as contaminated water, chemicals and infections. There also include bacterial infections such as brucellosis, which may persist for years; campylobacter jejune, which causes abdominal pain, fever, and diarrhea. Those infected suffer weight loss, fever, anemia, and enlargement of the spleen and liver. Severe mosquitoes bite also causes harm to their wellbeing.

Fig. 5.6: Physical strain during training among military personnel

Soldiers have used drugs to reduce pain, lessen fatigue, increase alertness, cope with boredom, or cope with the panic that accompanies battle. They may have started using drugs or alcohol in the service or developed a problem later in life. Substance abuse problems in veterans also may be linked with conditions such as post-traumatic stress disorder (PTSD). Substance abuse is highly correlated with post-traumatic stress disorder (PTSD) and other psychological disorder that may occur after stressful and traumatic events, because many trauma's result in physical injury, pain is often part of the experience of veterans. This physical pain often causes emotional distress, because in addition to causing pain and discomfort, the injury also reminds them of their trauma. Because traumas stress the body, they can sometimes affect physical health, and survivors may experience stress-related physical symptoms, such as headache, nausea or other stomach problems like peptic ulcers, diabetes, skin problems and sleep disturbances, changes in sleeping and appetite patterns. Some of the soldiers suffer from coronary heart diseases and other personal weakness. Military people face problems in high altitudes. Moreover, some people entering the military are more vulnerable to developing physical problems. Traumatic Brain injury (TBIs) includes cognitive issues such as shorter attention span, language disabilities, and an inability to process information. Sexual trauma that is associated with Military service most often occurs in a setting where the victim lives and works.

In most cases, this means that victims must continue to live and work closely with their perpetrators, often leading to an increased sense of feeling helpless, powerless, and at risk for additional victimization. Most Military groups are characterized by high unit cohesion, particularly during combat. While this level of solidarity typically reflects a positive aspect of Military service, the dynamics of cohesion may play a role in the negative psychological effects associated with sexual harassment and assault that occurs.

Fig. 5.7: Physical stress among the military personnel

PSYCHOLOGICAL PROBLEMS

The million strong force is under tremendous stress. In fact, the army is losing more soldiers in these incidents than in action against the enemy. Most experts attribute the growing stress to low morale, bad service conditions, lack of adequate home leave, and a communication gap with superiors. In addition family problems could also be factors. To counter suicides and other psychological problems, the commonest psychotic disorder amongst Indian Army is schizophrenia, alcohol dependence syndrome and neurotic depression, among other disorders driving the personnel to suicide and killing their own colleagues. Most persons who have been traumatized experience short term depression, it may involve feeling of helplessness and hopelessness, loss of pleasure in usual activities, lowers energy, pervasive and extreme sadness. May veterans blame themselves or feel guilty in some way. They may feel bad about something; they did or didn't do in the war zone. Feelings of guilt or self-blame cause much distress and can prevent a person from reaching out for help.

Fig. 5.8: Psychological problems during crisis situation

Severe psychological and physical symptoms can result from sudden, unexpected environmental crises. These severe symptoms often referred to as post-traumatic stress disorder (PTSD). PTSD includes elements of anxiety generalized feelings of fear and apprehension. Many soldiers who have been involved in the turmoil of war experience devastating psychological problems for months or even years afterward. It was gradually realized, however, that only a small percentage of such cases represented physical injury. Most victims were suffering instead from the general combat situation, with it physical fatigue, ever-present threat of death and mutilation, and severe psychological shocks. Even the latter terms were none too aptly chosen, because they implied that physical exhaustion played a more important role than was usually exhaustion. They did, however, serve to distinguish such disorders from other psychological disorders, such as drug use, that happened to occur under war conditions but might well have occurred in civilian life.

The specific symptoms of stress very considerably, are depending on the type of duty, severity and nature of the traumatic experience, and the personality of the individual. The anxiety levels of the civilians exposed to the threat of attack were significantly higher during the war than when they were retested after the war was over. The post-traumatic symptoms including intrusive imagery, hyper arousal, numbing, and cognitive disruption were associated with exposure to combat violence. Participation in abusive violence was not highly associated with more severe pathologies marked by cognitive disruptions such as depression. Combat involvement is also not the only stressor in a war zone. Soldiers involved in graves registration duties (e.g. handling corpses) had high rates of PTSD symptoms such as anger, anxiety, and somatic complaints compared with soldiers not assigned to such duties. Moreover, some people entering the military are more vulnerable to developing stress-related symptoms than others. Almost all veterans experience difficulty controlling distressing memories of military experiences, particularly when there has been combat experience. The first symptoms were increasing irritability and sensitivity, sleep disturbances, and often recurrent nightmares, difficulty falling or staying asleep and difficulty in concentrating. Sometimes they feel anxiety and panic attacks. The emotional numbing and feeling of disconnection that are common after traumatic events may

Fig. 5.9: Combat stress among the soldiers

create distress and drive a wedge between the survivor and his family or close friends. Some military personnel's and veterans have difficulty in experiencing loving or feeling some emotions, especially when upset by tragic memories.

The main difficulties faced by the Army personnel from psychological point of view is as follows:-

Loss of contact: *The individuals in Army develop a fear of losing contact with their near and dear ones duties the leave problems.*

Loss of individual's freedom: *The nature of job is such that it demands strict discipline and every activity are guided. This leaves the individual with the feeling of losing personal freedom.*

Feeling of loneliness and family worries: *The major cause driving personnel to commit suicide and some personal decide to end their lives when they visit their family and find them having difficulties in life. Living away from the family in difficult conditions makes them feel lonelier.*

Comparison with counterparts: *Many types of adjustment problems develop due to frustration when individual starts counterparts or is being compared by higher officials.*

Fear of death and getting wounded: *One of the most common fears which engulf the defense personnel is the fear of death. In spite of the fact that one day everyone has to die and the nature of army profession are such that this fact becomes more evident. But still fear of death keeps building up the stress. In many operations, soldiers get wounded and another fear crops up in the mind regarding the wound and the impairment or disability it will lead to.*

Fig. 5.10: Soldier showing the fear of defeat and death

Guilt feeling: *in spite of the hard training, many soldiers may suffer from guilt feeling of killing a fellow human being. However, the conscience should be clear that, he is doing so for a national cause.*

SOCIO-CULTURAL PROBLEMS

A number of social and interpersonal factors may contribute to the overall stress experienced by soldiers and predispose them to break down. Such factors include reductions in personal freedom, frustrations of all sorts, and separation from home and loved ones. The many stresses arising from combat including constant fear, unpredictable and largely uncontrollable circumstances, the necessity of killing, and prolonged harsh conditions.

Fig. 5.11: Adaptation of the soldiers in extreme environmental conditions

Personality is an important determinant of adjustment to military experiences. Personality characteristics that lower a person's resistance to stress or to particular stressors may be important in determining his reactions to combat. Some people are so accustomed to anxiety that they cope with it more or less automatically, whereas soldiers who are feeling severe anxiety for the first time may be terrified by the experience, lose their self-confidence, and panic.

Several socio-cultural factors play an important part in determining a person's adjustment to combat. Finally, if a soldier respects his leaders and officers, has confidence in their judgment and ability, figures, the soldiers moral and resistance to stress are bolstered. On the other hand, lack of confidence, or dislike of leaders is detrimental to moral and to tolerance to combat stress. It also appears that returning to an unaccepting to social environment can increase a soldier's vulnerability to post traumatic stress.

Fig. 5.12: Oath taking ceremony in military

Soldiers show extreme anxiety, depression, extensive physical complaints and self-harming behavior, but also that in many instances, they appear to have become more disturbed over time. The stressful events that veterans experience can also have a negative impact on their families when they return home.

CHAPTER

6

LIFE SATISFACTION AMONG MILITARY AND CIVILIAN PEOPLE

LIFE SATISFACTION AMONG MILITARY AND CIVILIAN PEOPLE

The average score of Himachali married people on the dimension of life satisfaction was 44.19, whereas the average score of Non-Himachali married people was 43.3. It shows that Himachali married people are much satisfied from their life as compare to their counterpart. Further the mean score of Himachali unmarried people on the parameter of life satisfaction was found as 37, whereas the average score of non-Himachali unmarried people was 33.38. It again shows that the Himachali unmarried people are much satisfied from their life as compare to their counterpart group.

Table-6.1

Average Score of Himachali and Non-Himachali Married and Unmarried Military and Civilian People on the Life Satisfaction Scale

Groups	Military	Civilian	Average
H.M	45.06	43.33	44.19
NH-M	43.93	42.13	43.03
H-UM	38.00	36.00	37.00
NH-UM	35.70	31.06	33.38
Average	46.72	38.13	39.4

Further average score of military people in the dimension of life satisfaction was 46.72. Whereas, of civilian was 38.13 in the same. It shows that military people are much satisfied from their life as compare to the civilian people. Similarly, the average score of Himachali married, military people was 45.06 on the dimension of life satisfaction whereas the average score of Himachali, married civil people was 43.33. It shows that Himachali married military people are much satisfied from their life as compare to their counterpart.

The mean score of Non-Himachali married, military people on the dimension of life satisfaction was 43.93, whereas the mean score of Non-Himachali, married, civil people on the dimension of life satisfaction was 42.13. It shows that Non-Himachali, married military people are much satisfied from their life as compare to the Non-Himachali, married, civil people. In the same time the average score of Himachali, unmarried, military people on the measure of life satisfaction was 38, whereas the average score of Himachali, unmarried, civil people was 36. It further shows that the Himachali, unmarried, military people are much satisfied from their life as compare to their counterpart. The mean score of Non-Himachali, unmarried, military people on the dimension of life satisfaction was 35.70, whereas the average score of the Non-Himachali unmarried civil people was 31.06. It shows that the Non-Himachali unmarried, military people are much satisfied from their life as compare to their counterpart.

The average score of Himachali, married, military people on the scale of life satisfaction was 45.06, whereas the average score of Non-Himachali, married, military people on the same dimension was 43.93. It shows that Himachali, married, military people are much satisfied from their life as compare to the counterpart. The average score of Himachali, married, military people on the life satisfaction dimension was 45.06 whereas the score of the Himachali unmarried, military people on the same dimension was 38. It shows that Himachali, married, military people are highly satisfied from their life as compare to the counterpart. The mean score of Himachali married, military person on the dimension of life satisfaction was 45.06, whereas the average score of Non-Himachali, unmarried, military people was 35.70. It shows that Himachali, married, military people are highly satisfied from their life as compare to their counterpart.

The average score of Non-Himachali, married, military people on the dimension of life satisfaction was 43.93, whereas the mean score of Himachali, unmarried military people on the life satisfaction was 38. It shows that Himachali, married, military people are much satisfied from their life as compare to their counterpart. The mean score of the con-Himachali married, military people on the life satisfaction scale was 43.93, whereas, the average score of non-Himachali, unmarried, military people was 35.70. It shows that the non-Himachali, married, military people are much satisfied from their life as compare to their counterpart. The average score of Himachali, unmarried, military people on the dimension of life satisfaction was 38, whereas the average score of

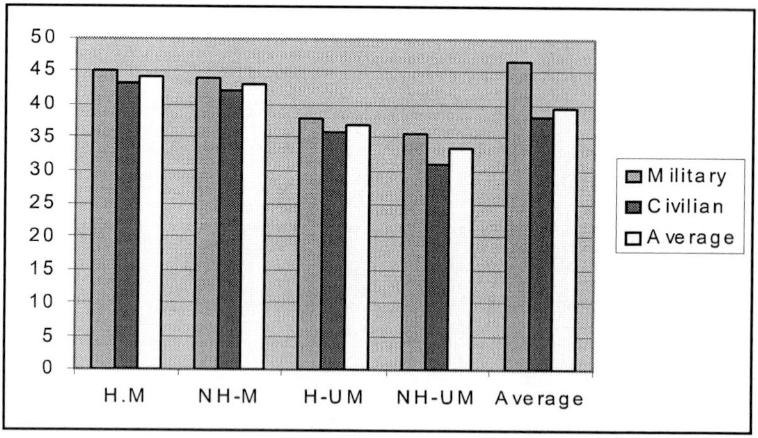

Fig. 6.1: Average Score of Himachali and Non-Himachali Married And Unmarried Military and Civilian People on The Life Satisfaction Scale

non-Himachali, unmarried military people was 35.70. It shows that the Himachali, unmarried, military people are much satisfied from their life as compare to their counterpart.

The average score of Himachali, married civilian people on the dimension of life satisfaction was 43.33, whereas the average score of non-Himachali, married, civilian people in the same dimension was 42.13. It further shows that Himachali, married, civilian people are slightly satisfied from their life as compare to their counterpart. Similarly the mean score of Himachali, married, civilian people on the life satisfaction scale was 43.33, whereas the mean score of Himachali, unmarried, civilian people on the same scale was 36. It shows that Himachali, married civilian people are much satisfied from their life as compare to the counterpart. The average score of Himachali, married, civilian people was 43.33, whereas, the average score of Non-Himachali, unmarried, civilian people was 31.06. It shows that the Himachali, married civilian people are much satisfied from their life as compare to the Non-Himachali, unmarried, civilian people.

The mean score of Non-Himachali, married, civilian people on the parameter of life satisfaction was 42.13, whereas the average score of Himachali, unmarried, civilian people on the same parameter was 36. It shows that the Non-Himachali, married, civilian people are much satisfied from their life as compare to their counterpart. The average score of Non-Himachali married, civilian people in the life satisfaction parameter was 42.13, whereas the mean score of Non-Himachali, unmarried, civilian people on the same parameter was 31.06. It again shows that Himachali, married civilian people are much satisfied from their life as compare to the Non-Himachali, unmarried, civilian people. The average score of Himachali, unmarried, civilian people on the dimension of life satisfaction was 36, whereas the average score on non-Himachali, unmarried, civilian people on the same dimension was 31.06. It shows that Himachali, unmarried, civilian people are much satisfied from their life as compare to their counterpart.

Military families like civilian one represent diversities with single parents and binuclear households. They dealt with stressful issues like finance, child and elderly care, physical and mental challenges. Their families are unique in facing the required challenge of tolerating and adapting to the multiple deployment and family separation. The human security concerns should be limited to situations marked by the threat or outbreak of violence. It is the root causes of conflict and requires a comprehensive approach (Shahrbanou, 2010). Mental health and wellbeing among military personnel is important for the effectiveness of nation's military, adjustment of their families and the integration of military personnel into the larger civilian community (Mark & Bowles, 2011). According to Goldenson (1984), mental health is a state of mind, characterized by emotional well-being, relative freedom from anxiety and disabling symptoms and a capacity to establish constructive relationship with ordinary demands and stresses of life. The study of Ikin, Sim, McKenzie, Horsley, Wilson, Harrex, et al. (2009) revealed that Korean War Veterans reported significantly lower Percentage Life Satisfaction (PLS) and quality of life scores on four WHOQOL-Bref domains, compared with similarly aged Australian men. Further, Bramsen, Deeg, Van der Ploeg, and Fransman (2007) studied late-life mortality among 1,448 World War II survivors. The highest hazard rates of mortality were found among military Veterans and war survivors. The study of Britt, Adler and Andrew (2010) reveals that the ethnic conflict has long lasting effect on health and wellbeing. The level of lifetime exposure to violence, the proportion of family members reporting pain and lifetime violence related injury and families' financial burden (Wang, Salihu, Rushiti, Bala & Modwig, 2010). The injured soldiers are less satisfied from their life compared to their counterpart (Linn, Linn, Segal, Sheps, Levi, & Revach, 2011).

SELF-ESTEEM AMONG MILITARY AND CIVILIAN PEOPLE

The average score of Himachali married people on the state self-esteem parameter was 76.73, whereas the average score of non-Himachali married people on the same parameter was 76.16. It shows that the Himachali married people showed slightly more self esteem as compare to their counterpart. Further the mean score of the Himachali unmarried people on the parameter of state self esteem was 77.73, whereas the average score of Non-Himachali unmarried people on the same dimension was 73.96. It shows that Himachali unmarried people exhibited much self-esteem as compare to their counterpart. The average score of military people on the state self-esteem dimension was 77.91, whereas of civilian people was 74.38 on the same parameter. It shows that military people reported more self-esteem as compare to their counterpart.

Table 6.2

Average Score of Himachali and Non-Himachali Married and Unmarried Military and Civilian People on the Self-Esteem Scale

Groups	Military	Civilian	Average
H.M	76.26	77.2	76.73
NH-M	75.93	76.4	76.16
H-UM	80.66	74.8	77.73
NH-UM	78.8	69.13	73.96
Average	77.91	74.38	76.145

The average score of Himachali married military people on the dimension of state self esteem was 76.26, whereas the average score of Himachali married civilian people on the same scale was 77.2. It shows that Himachali married civilian people were found slightly more in self-esteem as compare to their counterpart. Similarly the average score of Non-Himachali married military people on the parameter of state self esteem was 75.93, whereas the average score of non-Himachali married civilian people on the same dimension was 76.4. It shows that non-Himachali married civilian people were slightly more on self-esteem as compare to their counterpart. The mean score of Himachali unmarried military people on the dimension of state self esteem was 80.66, whereas the mean score of Himachali unmarried civilian people on the same parameter was 74.8. It shows that Himachali unmarried military people are higher in self esteem as compare to their counterpart. The mean score of non-Himachali unmarried military people on the dimension of state self esteem was 78.8, whereas the mean score of non-Himachali unmarried civilian people on the same dimension was 69.13. It shows that Himachali unmarried military people expressed high self esteem as compare to their counterpart.

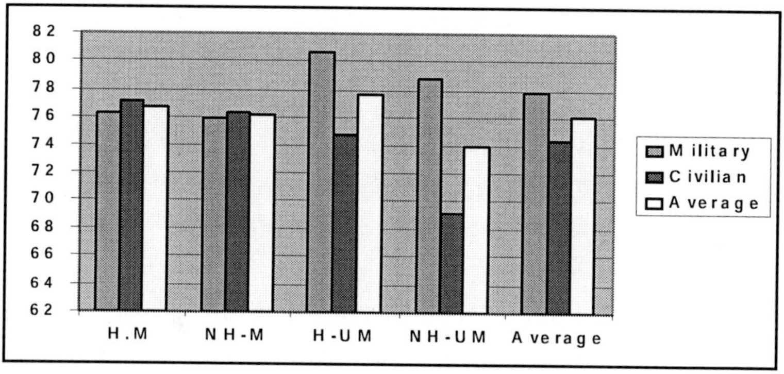

Fig 6.2: Average Score of Himachali and Non-Himachali Married and Unmarried Military and Civilian People on the Self-Esteem Scale

Further the average score of Himachali married military people on the parameter of state self esteem was 76.26, whereas the average score of non Himachali married military people on the same parameter was 75.93. It shows that Himachali married military people are more in self esteem as compare to the non Himachali married military people. The mean score of Himachali married military people on the scale of state self esteem was 76.26, whereas the mean score of Himachali unmarried military people on the dimension the average score of non Himachali unmarried military people on the dimension of state self esteem was 80.66. It shows that Himachali unmarried military people are having much self esteem as compare to their counterpart. The average score of Himachali married military people on the score of state self esteem was 76.26, whereas the average score of non Himachali unmarried military people on the same scale was 78.8. It shows that non Himachali unmarried military people reported much self esteem as compare to their counterpart. The mean score of non Himachali married military people on the dimension of state self esteem was 75.93, whereas the mean score of Himachali unmarried military people on the same parameter was 80.66. It shows that Himachali unmarried military people are having high self esteem as compare to their counterpart. The average score of non Himachali married military people on the dimension of state self esteem was 75.93, whereas the mean score of non Himachali unmarried military people on the same scale was 78.8. It shows that non Himachali unmarried military people are having much self esteem as compare to the non Himachali married military people. The average score of Himachali unmarried military people on the dimension of self esteem was 80.66, whereas the average score of non Himachali unmarried military people on the same dimension was78.8. It shows that Himachali unmarried military people were found high in self esteem as compare to their counterpart. The average score of Himachali married civilian people on the dimension of state self esteem was 77.2 whereas the mean score of non Himachali married civilian on the same parameter was 76.4. It shows that Himachali married civilian people were much in self esteem as compare to their counterpart. The average score of Himachali married civilian people on the dimension of state self esteem was 77.2 whereas the average score of Himachali unmarried civilian people on the same parameter was 74.8. It shows that Himachali married civilian people are having much self esteem as compare to their counterpart.

The average score of the Himachali married civilian people on the dimension of state self esteem was 77.2, whereas the average score of the non Himachali unmarried civilian people on the same scale was 69.13. It shows Himachali married civilian people are reported high degree of self esteem as compare to their counterpart. The mean score of the non Himachali married civilian people on the dimension of state self esteem was 76.4, whereas the mean score of the Himachali unmarried civilian people on the same dimension was 74.8. It shows that non Himachali married civilian showed much self esteem as compare to their counterpart. The average score of the non Himachali married civilian people on the state self esteem parameter was 76.4 whereas the average scores of non Himachali unmarried civilian people on the same scale was 69.13. It shows that non Himachali married civilian people have much self esteem as compare to their counterpart. The average score of Himachali unmarried civilian people on the dimension of self esteem was 74.8, whereas the average score of non Himachali unmarried civilian people on the same parameter was 69.13. It shows Himachali unmarried civilian people have high self esteem as compare to the non Himachali unmarried civilian people.

Ryff et al (1995), have proposed a theoretical model of well-being, which encompasses six distinct dimensions of wellness: 'autonomy', 'environment', 'mastery', 'personal growth', 'positive relation with others', 'purpose in life', and 'self-acceptance'. Spiro, Schnurr, and Aldwin (1997) points out that military service is a hidden variable in men's aging. The study of Schnurr, Spiro, Aldwin, and Stukel (1998) found no relationship with combat trauma and PTSD. WHO has recently proposed that mental health is a state of well-being in which the individual realizes his or her own abilities, can cope with the normal stresses of life, can work productively and fruitfully, and is able to make a contribution to his or her community (WHO, 2001, p.1). The external context of family is usually outside the control of the family and affect the family's perception of military separation therefore influence stress (Boss, 2002). Families' historical context of past family stress influence family management of stress (Cozolino, 2002). The social anxiety is uniquely associated with disturbunces in positive experiences, events, and traits (Todd, Terri, Keith, & Gitendra, 2006).

ALCOHOL, SMOKING AND SUBSTANCE INVOLVEMENT AMONG MILITARY AND CIVILIAN PEOPLE

The average score of Himachali married people on the dimension of substance abuse was4.45 whereas the score of non Himachali married people on the same dimension was 4.55. It shows that non Himachali married people are slightly more substance dependent as compare to their counterpart.

Table 6.3

Average Score of Himachali and Non-Himachali Married and Unmarried Civilian and Military people in Alcohol, Smoking and Substance

Groups	Military	Civilian	Average
H.M	5.6	3.3	4.45
NH-M	3.9	5.2	4.55
H-UM	5.9	4.13	5.01
NH-UM	4.2	7.4	5.8
Average	4.9	5.00	4.95

The average score of Himachali unmarried people on the same dimension of substance abuse was 5.15 whereas the average score of non Himachali unmarried people on the same dimension was 5.8. It shows that Himachali unmarried people are more substance dependent as compare to their counterpart. Further the average score of the military people on the same dimension of substance abuse was 4.9 whereas the average score of civilian people on the parameter of substance abuse was 5. It shows that civilian people are much substance dependent as compare to their counterpart group i.e. military people. The average score of the Himachali married military people o the dimension of substance abuse was 5.6 whereas the average score of the Himachali married civilian people on the same dimension was 3.3. It shows that Himachali married military people are more substance dependent as compare to their counterpart group. The average score of the non Himachali married military people on the dimension on the substance abuse scale was 3.9 whereas the average score of the non Himachali married civilian people on the same dimension was 5.2. It shows that non Himachali married civilian people are much substance dependent as compare to their counterpart. The average score of the Himachali unmarried military people on the parameter of substance abuse was 5.9 whereas the average score of the Himachali unmarried civilian people on the same parameter was 4.13. It shows that Himachali unmarried military people are much substance dependent as compare to their counterpart group.

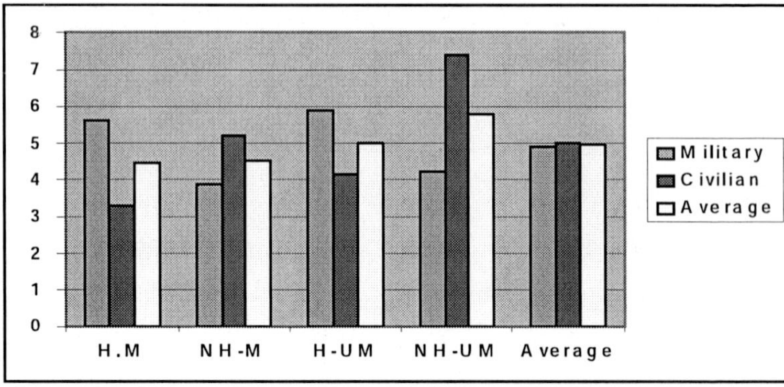

Fig. 6.3: Average Score of Himachali and Non-Himachali Married and Unmarried Civilian and Military people in Alcohol, Smoking and Substance

The average score of non Himachali unmarried military people on the dimension of substance abuse as 4.2 whereas the average score of non Himachali unmarried civilian people on the dimension of substance abuse was 7.4. It shows that Himachali unmarried civilian people are much substance dependent as compare to their counterpart. The mean score of the Himachali married military people on the dimension of substance abuse was 5.6 whereas the average score of the non Himachali married military people on the same parameter was 3.9. It shows that Himachali married military people are much substance dependent as compare to their counterpart group. The mean score of Himachali married military people on the dimension of substance abuse was 5.6 whereas the average score of the Himachali unmarried military people on the same dimension was 5.9. It shows the Himachali unmarried military people are much substance dependent as compare to their counterpart group. The mean score of the Himachali married military people on the dimension of substance abuse scale was 5.6 whereas the mean score of the non Himachali unmarried military people on the same dimension was 4.2. It shows that Himachali married military people are much substance dependent as compare to their counterpart group.

The mean score of non Himachali married military people on the substance abuse parameter was 3.9 whereas the average scores of Himachali unmarried military people on the same parameter was 5.9. It shows that Himachali unmarried military people are much substance dependent as compare to non Himachali married military people. The mean score of the non Himachali married military people on the parameter of substance abuse was 3.9 whereas the mean score of the non Himachali unmarried military people was 4.2. It shows that non Himachali unmarried military people are much substance dependent as compare to their counterpart. The average score of Himachali unmarried military people on the dimension of substance abuse was 5.9 whereas the average score of non Himachali unmarried military people on the same scale was 4.2. It shows that Himachali unmarried military people are much substance dependent as compare to their counterpart group.

The average score of Himachali married civilian people on the dimension of substance abuse was 3.3 whereas the average score of non Himachali married civilian people on the same parameter was 5.2. It shows that non Himachali married civilian people are much substance dependent as compare to their counterpart. The average score of Himachali married civilian people on the dimension of substance abuse was 3.3 whereas the mean score of Himachali unmarried civilian people on the same parameter was 4.13. It shows that Himachali unmarried civilian people are much substance dependent as compare to their counterpart group. The average score of the Himachali married civilian people on the substance abuse scale was 3.3 whereas the average score of non Himachali unmarried civilian people on the same dimension was 7.4. It shows that non Himachali unmarried civilian people are much substance dependent as compare to their counterpart group. The mean score of the non Himachali married civilian people on the substance abuse dimension was 5.2 whereas the mean score of the Himachali married civilian people on the same scale was 4.13. It shows that non Himachali married civilian people are much substance dependent as compare to their counterpart. The mean score of the non Himachali unmarried civilian people on the parameter of substance abuse was 5.2 whereas the mean score of non Himachali unmarried civilian people on the same parameter was 7.4. It shows that non Himachali unmarried civilian people are much substance dependent as compare to their counterpart. The average score of Himachali unmarried civilian people on the dimension of substance abuse was 4.13 whereas the average score of non Himachali unmarried civilian people on the same dimension was 7.4. It shows that non Himachali unmarried civilian people are much dependent as compare to non Himachali married civilian people. No single definition of "normal" drinking, problem drinking, or alcohol dependence can apply equally to all countries or cultures (Bennett, Campillo, Chandrashekar, & Gureje, 1998).

WELL-BEING AMONG CIVILIAN AND MILITARY PEOPLE

The average score of Himachali married people on the dimension of PGI General Well-being was 17.35, whereas the average score of Non Himachali married people on the same parameter was 17.35. It shows that the both groups are having same well being. The average score of Himachali unmarried people on the dimension of PGI General well being measure was 17.06, whereas the average score of Non Himachali unmarried people on the same dimension was 15.93. It shows that Himachali unmarried people are reported better well-being as compare to their counterpart. The average score of military people on the dimension of PGI General well being measure was 17.89, whereas the average score of civilian people on the PGI well being measure on the same parameter was 15.94. It shows that military people are having better well being as compare to their counterpart group. The mean score of Himachali married military people on the dimension of PGI General well being was 17.9, whereas the mean score of Himachali married civilian people in the same dimension was 16.8.

Table 6.4

Average Score of Himachali and Non-Himachali Married and Unmarried Military and Civilian People on General Wellbeing

Groups	Military	Civilian	Average
H.M	17.9	16.8	17.35
NH-M	17.5	17.2	17.35
H-UM	18.06	16.06	17.06
NH-UM	18.13	13.73	15.93
Average	17.89	15.94	16.92

It shows that Himachali married military people are having better well being as compare to their counterpart. The mean score of non Himachali married military people on dimension of PGI General well being measure was 17.5, whereas the average score of non Himachali married civilian people on the same scale was 17.2. It shows that non Himachali married military people are having better were being as compare to their counterpart group. The average score of Himachali unmarried military people on the measure of PGI general well-being was 18.06, whereas the average score of Himachali unmarried civilian people on the same parameter were 16.06. It shows that Himachali unmarried military people are having better well being as compare to the Himachali unmarried civilian people. The average score of non Himachali unmarried military people on the dimension of PGI General well being was 18.13 whereas the average score of Non Himachali unmarried civilian people on the same scale was 13.73. It shows that non Himachali unmarried military people are having better well being as compare to their counterpart group.

The average score of Himachali married military people on the measure of PGI General well being was 17.9, whereas the average score of non Himachali married military people on the same dimension was 17.5. It shows that Himachali married military people are having better general well being as compare to their counterpart. The average score of Himachali married military people on the dimension of PGI General well being was 17.9, whereas the mean score of Himachali unmarried military people on the same parameter

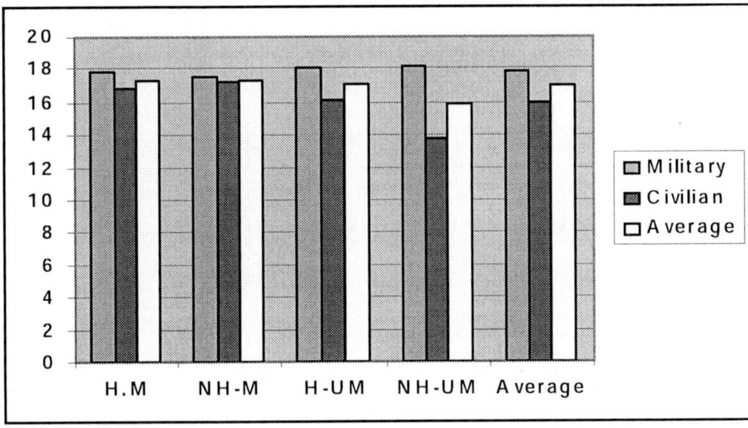

Fig. 6.4 Average Score of Himachali and Non-Himachali Married and Unmarried Military and Civilian People on general wellbeing

was 18.06. It shows that Himachali unmarried military people are having better well being as compare to their counterpart group. The mean score of Himachali married military people on the measure of PGI General well being was 17.9 whereas the mean score of non Himachali unmarried military people on the same scale was 18.13. It shows that non Himachali unmarried military people are having better well being as compare to their counterpart group. The average score of non Himachali married military people on the parameter of PGI General well being was 17.5, whereas the mean score of Himachali unmarried military people on the same parameter was 18.06. It shows that Himachali unmarried military people are having better well being as compare to their counterpart.

The average score of non Himachali married military people on the measure of PGI General well being was 17.5, whereas the average score of non Himachali unmarried military people on the same parameter was 18.13. It shows that non Himachali unmarried military people are having better well being as compare to their counterpart. The average score of Himachali unmarried military people on the measure of PGI General well being was 18.06, whereas the mean score of non Himachali unmarried military people on the same parameter was 18.13. It shows that non Himachali unmarried military people are having better well being as compare to their counterpart group.

The average score of Himachali married civilian people on the measure of PGI General well being was 16.8, whereas the average score of non Himachali married civilian people on the same parameter was 17.2. It shows that non Himachali married civilian people are having better well being as compare to their counterpart group. The average score of Himachali married civilian people on the measure of PGI General well being was 16.8, whereas the average score of Himachali unmarried civilian people on the same parameter was 16.06. It shows that Himachali married civilian people are having better well being as compare to their counterpart. The mean score of Himachali married civilian people on the parameter on PGI General well being measure was 16.8, whereas the mean score of non Himachali unmarried civilian people on the same scale was 13.73. It shows that Himachali married civilian people are having better well being as compare their counterpart group. The mean score of non Himachali married civilian people on the parameter of PGI General well being measure was 17.2 whereas the average score of Himachali unmarried civilian people on the same dimension was 16.06. It shows that Himachali married civilian people are having better well being as compare to

Himachali unmarried civilian people. The mean score of Non-Himachali married civilian people on the measure of PGI General well being was 17.2, whereas the mean score of on Himachali unmarried civilian people on the same dimension was 13.73. It shows that non Himachali married civilian people are having better well being as compare to their counterpart. The mean score of Himachali unmarried civilian people on the dimension of PGI General well being was 16.06 whereas the average score of Non-Himachali unmarried civilian people on the same dimension was 13.73. It shows that Himachali unmarried civilian people are having better well being as compare to their counterpart group.

The study of Zeiss and Dickman (1989) PTSD is a highly persistent phenomenon and that both situation and person variables contribute to the development and maintenance of PTSD. More than 1.6 million military men and women have deployed to fight the global war on terror. The studies of Vietnam Veterans demonstrate the negative impact on families of war-related PTSD. These Veterans have higher levels of marital problems, family violence, and partner distress. Their children present more behavioral problems than do those of Veterans without PTSD (Kulka, Schlenger, Fairbank, Hough, Jordan, Marmar, et al. , 1990). Neither mental nor physical health can exist alone. Mental, physical and social functioning is interdependent but health and illness may co-exist (Sartorius, 1990). Hall and Jansen (1995) found increased levels of arousal in officers and older soldiers. Higher levels of arousal were also found in subjects reporting a greater numbers of hours of sleep during the preceding 24 hours. WHO and other international organizations identify the improvement of mental health as a priority concern for low and middle income countries as well as for wealthier nations and people (WHO, 2001b). The military recruitment is directed associated with their health which is defined as a state of complete physical, mental and social well-being of a person not merely the absence of disease or infirmity (WHO, 2001b, p.1). The study conducted by Kang, Bullman, & Taylor, (2006) that those PoWs with PTSD also had statistically significant increased risks of cardiovascular diseases including hypertension and chronic ischemic heart disease when compared to both non-POWs and POWs without PTSD. The parental deployment affect school going children (Eric, Flake, Patti, & Laura, 2009). Military, family and community supports help mitigate family stress during periods of deployment (Eric, Flake, Patti, & Laura S. 2009). Mmari, Bradshaw, & Sudhinaraset (2010) on 11 focal military youth groups the parents and youths who have better social connectedness are well adjusted compared to their counterpart. Sudin, Fear, HullJones, Dandekar, Hotof, Wessely, and Rona (2010) deployment experience and subsequently feel positive and negative stress. The deployment is directly related to the acute stress reaction and adjustment disorders (Alyssa, Jay, Stephen, Bradley, Joseph, Charles, & Engel, 2010).

DEPRESSION AMONG MILITARY AND CIVILIAN PEOPLE

The average score of Himachali married people on the Beck's Depression inventory was 14.03, whereas the average score of Non-Himachali married people on the same dimension was 12.16. It shows that Himachali married people feels much depression as compare to their counterpart. The average score of Himachali unmarried people on the dimension of Beck's depression inventory was 11.79, whereas the average score of non Himachali unmarried people on the same parameter was 12.33. It shows that non Himachali unmarried people feels much depression as compare to their counterpart. The average score of military people on the dimension of Beck's Depression was found as 10.06 whereas; the mean score of civilian people on the parameter of Beck's Depression inventory was 15.09.

Table 6.5

Average score of Himachali and Non-Himachali Married and Unmarried Military and Civilian People on BDI

Groups	Military	Civilian	Average
H.M	11.66	16.4	14.03
NH-M	7.4	16.93	12.16
H-UM	13.33	10.26	11.79
NH-UM	7.86	16.8	12.33
Average	10.06	15.09	12.57

It shows that the civilian people feel much depression as compare to their counterpart group. The average score of Himachali married military people on the parameter of Beck's Depression inventory was 11.66, whereas the average score of Himachali married civilian people on the same dimension was 16.4. It shows that Himachali married civilian people feels much depression as compare to their counter group. The average score of Non-Himachali married military people on the dimension of Beck's Depression inventory was found as 7.4, whereas the average score of non Himachali married civilian on the same parameter was 16.93. It shows that non Himachali married civilian people feels much depression as compare to the non-Himachali married military people. The mean score of Himachali unmarried military people on Beck's depression inventory was 13.33, whereas the average score of Himachali unmarried civilian people on the same inventory was 10.26. It shows that Himachali unmarried military people feels much depression as compare to their counterpart group. The mean score of Non Himachali unmarried military people on the parameter of Beck's Depression inventory was found as 7.86, whereas the average score of non Himachali unmarried civilian people on the same parameter as 16.8. It shows that non Himachali unmarried civilian people feels much depression as compare to their counterpart group.

The average score of Himachali married military people on the Beck's Depression Inventory was 11.66, whereas the average score of non Himachali married military people on the same inventory was 7.4. It shows that Himachali married military people feels much depression as compare to their counterpart group. The mean score of Himachali married military people on Beck's Depression Inventory was 11.66, whereas the mean score of Himachali unmarried military people on the same scale was 13.33. It shows that Himachali unmarried military people feels much depression as compare to their counterpart. The average score of Himachali married military people on the inventory of Beck's Depression was found as 11.66, whereas the average score of non Himachali unmarried military people on the same parameter was 7.86.

It shows that Himachali married military people feels much depression as compare to their counterpart group.

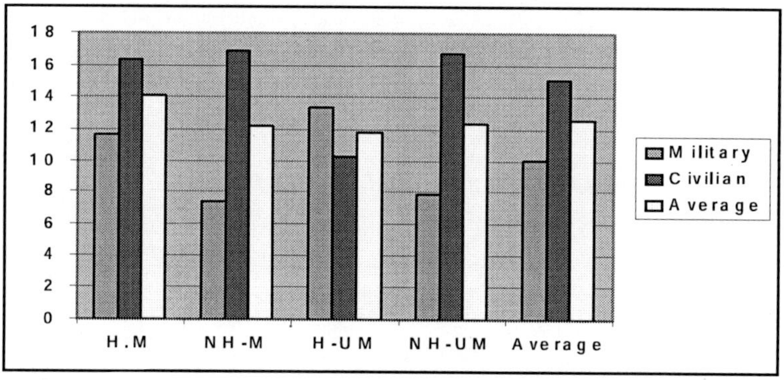

Fig. 6.5: Average score of Himachali and Non-Himachali Married and Unmarried Military and Civilian People on BDI

The average score of non Himachali married military people on Beck's depression inventory was 7.4, whereas the mean score of Himachali unmarried military people on the same dimension was 13.33. It shows that Himachali unmarried military people feels much depression as compare to their counterpart group. The mean score of Non Himachali married military people on Beck's depression Inventory was 7.4, whereas the mean score of Non Himachali unmarried military people on the same dimension was 7.86. It shows that non himachali unmarried military people feels much depression as compare to their counterpart. The average score of Himachali unmarried military people on the dimension of Beck's depression was 13.33, whereas the average score of non Himachali unmarried military people on the same dimension was 7.86. It shows that Himachali unmarried military people feels more depression as compare to their counterpart.

The average score of Himcahali married civilian people on the dimension of Beck's Depression inventory found as 16.4, whereas the average score of non Himachali married civilian people on the same dimension was 16.93. It shows that non Himachali married civilian people feels much depression as compare to their counterpart group. The mean score of Himachali married civilian people on the parameter of Beck's Depression inventory was found as 15.4, whereas the average score of Himachali unmarried civilian people in the same parameter was 10.26. It shows that Himachali married civilian people feels more depression as compare to their counterpart. The mean score of Himachali married civilian people on Beck's depression inventory was found as 16.4, whereas the mean score of Non Himachali unmarried civilian people on the same scale was 16.8 depression. It shows that non Himachali unmarried civilian people feels much as compare to their counterpart. The average score of Non Himachali married civilian people on the inventory of Beck's Depression was 16.93, whereas the average scores of Himachali unmarried civilian people on same parameter was 10.26. It shows that non Himachali married civilian people feels more depression as compare to their counterpart group. The mean score of Non Himachali married civilian people on the dimension of Beck's Depression was 16.93, whereas the mean score of Non Himachali unmarried civilian people on the same parameter was 16.8. It shows that non Himachali married civilians feels much depression as compare to their counterpart. The average score of Himachali unmarried civilian people on the dimension of Beck's Depression was 10.25, whereas the average score of Non Himachali unmarried civilian people on the parameter of Beck's Depression was found as 16.8. It clearly shows that non Himachali unmarried civilian people feels more depression as compare to their counterpart group i.e. Himachali unmarried civilian people.

Military deployment and duty related separation are defining experience for military services member and their families. They are one of the most widely recognized and documented stressors for military families (Albano, 1994; Black, 1993; Drumet, Coleman & Cable, Kelly et al, 2001; Orthner, 2002; Orthner, Bowen, & Beare, 1990; Vormbrock, 1993). There is higher prevalence of major depression, generalized anxiety, or PTSD among the soldier who fought battle in Iraq (Charles, Carl, Stephen, Dennis, Dave, & Robert L. 2004). Fiedler, Ozakinci, Hallman, Wartenberg, Brewer, Barrett, and Kiepen (2006) found military deployment to the gulf war as a risk factor for psychiatric illness among us troop. After injuries in the war the military personnel has to undergo with various psychological trauma (Hugh & de Girolambo, 2007).

Younger groups were more prone towards receiving mental health services (Seal, Bertenthal, Miner, Sen, & Marmar, 2007). The study of Jose, Donald, and Mark (2007) provides a framework for considering the global burden of illness attributable to dengue, and its cost, and describes challenges encountered in the estimation of these values. Focus on LOC perspective itself is the cause of anxiety (Al-Turkait, & Ohaeri, 2008). The study of Chandra and Martin (2009) observed that military families have experienced multiple and extended deployments stress. The interaction between meaning in life and depression also was significant, with a stronger inverse relation between meaning and PTSD at lower levels of depression. Meaning in life may be an important treatment concern for veterans with PTSD symptoms, particularly at higher levels of functioning (Owens, Steger, Whitesell & Herrera, 2009). A study was conducted by Herzog, Everson, and Whitworth (2011) reveals that immediate family member of combat exposed soldiers with high level of were at risk of developing secondary traumatic stress.

An efforts should be made to eliminate alcohol abuse should be intensified (Robert & Mary, 1992). Cannon-Bowers, Salas, Tannenbaumscott, & Mathew, 1995). Ballone 2000 focuses on peacekeeping operations.Further educational approach is required for enhancing self-esteem in the WTU cadre (Hammermeister, Michael & Carl, 2009). UK are initiating projects that connect returning soldiers to nature, through gardening, farming, job skills, hunting, fishing, retreat centers, camps, and outdoor adventure experiences to promote their wellbeing (Tidball, & Marianne, 2010). The study focuses on increasing soft power in India's foreign policy (Purushothaman, 2010). National security is the requirement to maintain the survival of the state through the use of economic, power projection and political power and the exercise of diplomacy. The origin of the modern concept of "national security" as a philosophy of maintaining a stable nation state can be traced to the Peace of Westphalia, wherein the concept of a sovereign state, ruled by a sovereign, became the basis of a new international order of nation states

(Haftendorn, 1991). The study of Murithi (2006) examines African indigenous approaches e.g. building social solidarity to building peace and promoting social solidarity. It will begin by looking at the reasons why it is necessary to build peace. Parkkari, et al. (2011) found neuromuscular training program with injury prevention counseling is effective in preventing acute musculoskeletal injuries in young men during military service. The social resilience through an educational, computer-based program may increase their wellbeing (John, Harry, & Alex, 2011).

CONCLUSION

The objective of the present study is to compare the Military personnel and Civilian on the dimensions of psychological wellbeing (Life satisfaction, wellbeing, self-esteem, depression, alcohol, smoking and substance uses). Further the study also intends to identify the difference between married and unmarried military personnel and civilians on various dimension of psychological wellbeing (Life satisfaction, wellbeing, self-esteem, depression, alcohol, smoking and substance uses). Similarly the study further makes out the difference between Himachali and Non-Himachali married and unmarried military personnel and civilians on various dimension of psychological wellbeing (Life satisfaction, wellbeing, self-esteem, depression, alcohol, smoking and substance uses). For accomplishing the objective the study has been conducted on a sample of N=120 those were divided into two sub-groups based on their profession i.e. from Military (N=60) and civil (N=60). These subjects were again sub-divided into two comparable half based on their marital status that comprises of N=30 married as well as another N=30 unmarried. Finally, the subjects were divided into two comparable half based on their domicile that comprises of N=15 Himachali as well as another N=15 non-Himachali. In all, there were eight groups with N=15 subjects in each that comprise of a complete sample of 120 subjects of aforesaid characteristics. Thus A 2 x 2 x 2 factorial design was used. These eight groups were assessed with the help of qualitative and quantitative measures. The qualitative measure include, field observation, interview, fuzzy cognitive mapping and photography whereas the quantitative measure include the life satisfaction scale, state self-esteem scale, Alcohol, smoking, substance involvement screening test, PGI General well-being measure and Beck's depression inventory. The quantitative measure is self-report in nature that was administered by the researcher herself by asking open ended question, from the participants. Since the researcher herself dealt with Subathu area of district Solan, therefore, it helped a lot in asking questions to the local dialects from the civilians while carrying out descriptive information's. Beside this the researcher did her pilot study and asked various people about the problems in military. The researcher entered in the particular area, by establishing warmth atmospheres with the participants followed with addressing the goal.

The ideas elicited by the subjects were welcomed by the researcher and they were encouraged to explain more about the problems in military. The researcher used observation, interview, fuzzy cognitive mapping as well as photography to record the life of the army personnel. Though qualitative analysis their view were record and described in the result section. Beside this the subjects were analyzed though life satisfaction scale, state self-esteem scale, alcohol smoking substance involvement screening test, PGI General well-being measure and Beck's 'depression inventory in order to record qualitative data about the psycho-socio issues in military so as to verify the dependent variable justified and scientifically. Their scores were tabulated and means were compared and analyzed by performing three way analysis of variance.

The average score of Himachali married people on the dimension of life satisfaction was 44.19, whereas the average score of Non-Himachali married people was 43.3. It shows that Himachali married people are much satisfied from their life as compare to their counterpart. Further the mean score of Himachali unmarried people on the parameter of life satisfaction was found as 37, whereas the average score of non-Himachali unmarried people was 33.38. It again shows that the Himachali unmarried people are much satisfied from their life as compare to their counterpart group. Further average score of military people in the dimension of life satisfaction was 46.72. Whereas, of civilian was 38.13 in the same. It shows that military people are much satisfied from their life as compare to the civilian people. The average score of Himachali married people on the state self-esteem parameter was 76.73, whereas the average score of non-Himachali married people on the same parameter was 76.16. It shows that the Himachali married people showed slightly more self-esteem as compare to their counterpart. Further the mean score of the Himachali unmarried people on the parameter of state self-esteem was 77.73, whereas the average score of Non-Himachali unmarried people on the same dimension was 73.96. It shows that Himachali unmarried people exhibited much self-esteem as compare to their counterpart. The average score of military people on the state self-esteem dimension was 77.91, whereas of civilian people was 74.38 on the same parameter. It shows that military people reported more self-esteem as compare to their counterpart.

The average score of Himachali married people on the dimension of substance abuse was 4.45 whereas the score of non Himachali married people on the same dimension was

4.55. It shows that non Himachali married people are slightly more substance dependent as compare to their counterpart. The average score of Himachali unmarried people on the same dimension of substance abuse was 5.15 whereas the average score of non Himachali unmarried people on the same dimension was 5.8. It shows that Himachali unmarried people are more substance dependent as compare to their counterpart. Further the average score of the military people on the same dimension of substance abuse was 4.9 whereas the average score of civilian people on the parameter of substance abuse was 5. It shows that civilian people are much substance dependent as compare to their counterpart group i.e. military people.

The average score of Himachali married people on the dimension of PGI General Well-being was 17.35, whereas the average score of Non Himachali married people on the same parameter was 17.35. It shows that the both groups are having same well-being. The average score of Himachali unmarried people on the dimension of PGI General Well-being measure was 17.06, whereas the average score of Non Himachali unmarried people on the same dimension was 15.93. It shows that Himachali unmarried people are reported better well-being as compare to their counterpart. The average score of military people on the dimension of PGI General Well-being measure was 17.89, whereas the average score of civilian people on the PGI well-being measure on the same parameter was 15.94. It shows that military people are having better well-being as compare to their counterpart group. The average score of Himachali married people on the Beck's Depression inventory was 14.03, whereas the average score of Non-Himachali married people on the same dimension was 12.16. It shows that Himachali married people feels much depression as compare to their counterpart. The average score of Himachali unmarried people on the dimension of Beck's depression inventory was 11.79, whereas the average score of non Himachali unmarried people on the same parameter was 12.33. It shows that non Himachali unmarried people feels much depression as compare to their counterpart. The average score of military people on the dimension of Beck's Depression was found as 10.06 whereas; the mean score of civilian people on the parameter of Beck's Depression inventory was 15.09. It shows that the civilian people feel much depression as compare to their counterpart group.

SUGGESTIONS

1. *Since the soldiers all the time are ready to fight and become martyred for the sake of their motherland therefore this behaviour be reinforced properly through proper incentive, emoluments and increasing their salary twice than that of their counterpart civilian or employees working in other sectors.*
2. *Beside improving physical health due importance be given to increase their psychological health that include their inner beliefs, cognitive processes, perceptions, motivations, attention, personality as well as behaviour that may include their action and reactions.*
3. *Further social-relationship and connectivity needs to be rejuvenated through community gathering along with civilians. The cultural discrimination and prejudices during their operation in general and service time in particular need to be conditioned.*
4. *The Defense Ministry/Home Ministry should release appropriate funds to update and upgrade their weapons, tanks, missiles, grenade, fighter planes, steamers etc. The country should become atomic power for the sake of providing security to the people.*
5. *Besides facilitating the soldiers with physical weapons there is a need to empower them psychologically that is only possible by enhancing their capability, capacities and abilities.*
6. *Enhancement of capability is only possible with the consultation of professional such as psychologists and counselor. Beside this the soldier is encouraged for higher education along with full salary so as to mitigate mind war. The technological education be imparted to them and special workshop/seminar and conferences in that context be provided to them.*
7. *Spiritual counselling is also required because all power is controlled by Supreme Being. The belief in local deities and devta further can improve their skill during operations.*

Such practices also need the help of professional such as Para psychologists.

8. *Special quotas or reservation be provided to the soldier in general after completing their job and their children and family members in particular.*
9. *After tiring task the soldier is given refreshment and tours be organized for the same. Further they are allowed to go wherever they want to go in that locality where they are recruited.*
10. *Since the era is of information and technology, the soldiers be allowed to do email, use telephone and mobile as well as watch movies in theatre.*
11. *Those soldiers who aspire to pass their marital life they be facilitated by exploring bride by contacting in locality or giving matrimonial advertisement so as to vanish their anxiety.*
12. *Further the soldier be honest, disciplined, hard worker and follower of his boss. The immediate boss should also avoid favoritism against them.*
13. *Psychological and counselling practices to overcome stress and anxiety that may include consciousness and awareness of things; practice of being positive in your thoughts and actions; developing your tact, modifying behaviour, trait, habits and actions (e.g. courteous and cheerful gesture); understanding and actualizing yourself, strong will power and enthusiasm; better conduct; self-discipline and calmness may help a lot. Further habit og alert and good listener; develop endurance and patience and listening music and avoiding argument and panic situation may help them. Behaviour modification technique, Self-actualization and humanistic approach and cognitive and behaviour modification as well as practice of yoga and medication followed with regular exercises may prove as assets for maintaining their wellbeing.*

14. *Therefore, there is a need of of psychologist, dietician and counselling psychologists to overcome their physical, social-cultural and psychological problems.*
15. *Special emphasis is given to recruit permanent psychologist in every wing so as to maintain and restore mental and behavioural disorder faced by the soldiers from time to time.*

REFERENCES

Ahmad, A., Reza, T., Hormoz, S., & Aliakbar, K. (2007). Knowledge of hospital infection control by supervisors in three selected Military Hospitals in Islamic Republic of Iran. Tehran: Department of Health services Management, School of Health Baqyiatallah Medical Sciences University.

Ahronson, A., Cameron, J. E. (2007). The nature and consequences of group cohesion in military sample. *Military Psychology, 19,* 9-25.

Ainsworth, M. (1989). Attachment beyond infancy. *American Psychologists, 44,* 409-716.

Albano, S. (1994). Military recognition of family concerns: Revolutionary War to 1993. *Armed Forces & Society, 20(2),* 283-303.

Alexander R. D. (2011). The global participant-oObserver: Emergence, challenges and opportunities. *The Public Sector Innovation Journal, 16(1),* article 9.

Al-Turkait, F. A. & Ohaeri, J. U. (2008). Prevalence and correlates of posttraumatic stress disorder among Kuwaiti military men according to level of involvement in the first Gulf War *Depress Anxiety, 25(11),* 932-41.

Alyssa, J. M. , Jay, S. K., Stephen, W. M., Bradley, N. G., Joseph, P. M., Charles, C., Engel, M.D., (2010). Deployment and the Use of Mental Health Services among U.S. Army Wives New England *Journal of Medicine,* 362, 101-109.

American Psychiatric Association (1994). *Diagnostic and statistical manual of mental disorder* (4th Ed.). Washington, DC.

Ames, G.M., and Grube, J.W. Alcohol availability & workplace drinking: Mixed method analysis. *Journal of Studies on Alcohol,* 60, 383-393.

Anderson, B. J. (1987). *Re-integration and re-adjustment program for officers returning from deployment in Iraq and Afghanistan.* Metropolitan Police Department Washington, DC.

Ballone, E. (2000). Factors Influencing Psychological Stress levels of Italian Peacekeepers in Bosnia. Military Medicine, 65, 911-915.

Bandura, A. (1986). Social foundation of thought and action: A social cognitive theory. Englewood cliffs, NJ: Prentice Hall.

Bandura, A. (1989). Human agency in social cognitive theory. American Psychologist, 44 (9), 175-1184.

Bandura, A. (1997). Self-efficacy: The exercise of control. New York: W.H. Freeman.

Bandura, A., Barbaranelli, C. Caprara, G.V., & Pastorelli, C. (2001). Self-efficacy beliefs as shapers of children's aspirations and career trajectories. Child Development, 72(1), 187-206.

Bandura, A., Locke, E. A. (2003). Negative self-efficacy and goal-effects revisited. Journal of Applied Psychology, 88 (1), 87-99.

Banton, R., Clifford, P.Frosh, S., Lusada, J. & Rosenthall, J. (1985), The politics of mental health. London: Macmillan.

Barber, B. & Schluterman, J. (2008). Connectedness in the lives of children and adolescence. A call for greater conceptual clarity. Journal of Adolescence Health, 43(3), 209-216.

Basham, K. & Miehls, D. (2004). Transforming the legacy: Couple therapy with survivors of child trauma. New York: Columbia University

Basham, K. (2008). Homecoming as safe heaven or the new front: Attachment and detachment in military couples. Clinical Social Work, 36, 83-96.

Batten, S.V., Drapalski, A.L., Decker, M.L., Deviva, J.C., Morris, L.J., Mann, M.A. et al. (2009). Veteran interest in family involvement in PTSD treatment. Psychological Services, 6(3), 184-189.

Beam, M. R., Chen, C., & Greenberger, E. (2002). The nature of adolescent relationship with their "very important" non-parental adults. American Journal of Community Psychology, 30, 305-325.

Bennett, L.A., Campillo, C., Chandrashekar, C.R. & Gureje, O.(1998). Alcoholic beverage consumption in India, Mexico, and Nigeria: A cross-cultural comparison, *Literature Review, 22 (4).*

Bertell, R. (2001). *Planet earth: The latest weapon of war.* MacBride Peace Prize winner.

Black W. (1993). Military induced family separation: A stress reduction intervention. *Social Work, 38,* 273-280.

Boss, P., Covden, B.A. (2002). Ambigous loss from chronic physical illness: Clinical interventions with individuals, couples and families. *Journal of Clinical Psychology, 58(11),* 1351-1360.

Bowlby, J. (1969.73/82). *Attachment and loss: Separation, anxiety and anger.* New York: *Basic Books.*

Bowlby, J. (1988). *A secure base: clinical application of attachment theory.* London: Routeledge.

Bradburn N.M. Caplovitz, P (1965). *Reports on happiness: A pilot study of behavior-related to mental health.* Chicago: Aldine.

Bramsen, I., Deeg, D.J.H., Van der Ploeg, E., & Fransman, S. (2007). Wartime stressors and mental health symptoms as predictors of late-life mortality in World War II survivors. *Journal of Affective Disorders, 103,* 121-129.

Britt, T. W., Adler, A. B., & Bartone, P. T. (2007). Deriving benefit from stressful events: The role of engagement in meaningful work and hardiness. *Journal of Occupational Health Psychology, 12,* 34-47.

Britt, T.W., Adler A.B. & Castro, C.A. (2006). Military Life: The Psychology of serving in peace and combat, 1, Santa Barbara, CA: Greenwood Publishing Group.

Britt, T.W., Adler, A.B. & P.T. Bartone (2001). Deriving benefits from stressful events: The role of engagement in meaningful work and hardiness. *Journal of Occupational Health Psychology, 6,* 53-63.

Browne, T., Hull, L., Horn, O, Jones, M., Murphy, D., Fear, N. T., Greenberg, N., French, C., Rona, R. J., Wessely, S., & Hotopf, M. (2007). Explanation for the increase in mental health problem in UK reserve force who have served in Iraq . British Journal of Psychiatry, 190, 484-489.

Cannon-Bowers, J. A., Salas, E., Tannenbaumscott, I., & Mathew, J. E. (1995). Towards theoretically based principles of training effectiveness: A model, and initial empirical investigation. Military Psychology, 7(3), 141-164.

Carmen G. Arroyo, C.G. & Zigler, E. (1995). Racial identity, academic achievement, and the psychological well-being of economically disadvantaged adolescents. Journal of Personality & Social Psychology, 69, (5), 903-914.

Carol D.Ryff, C.D., & Keyes, C.L.M. (1995). The structure of Psychological *well-being revisited. Journal of Personality and social psychology,* 69, 4, *719-727.*

Centre for International Cooperation and Security Department of Peace *(2005). The impact of armed violence on poverty and development.* Report *of the Armed Violence and Poverty Initiative.*

CFCP (1965). Editorial, 23 Nov., FE, 2, 2022.

Champion, H. R., Bellami, R. F., Roberts, P., & Leppaneimi, A. (2003). A profile of combat injury. Journal of Trauma, 54, 13-19.

Chandra, A. & Martin, L. T. (2009). The Impact of parental d deployment on child social and emotional wellbeing. Society for Adolescent Medicine.

Charles W. H., Carl, A. C., Stephen, C. M., Dennis, M. G. , Dave, I. C. & Robert L. K. (2004). Combat duty in Iraq and Afghanistan, mental health problems, and barriers to care. New England Journal of Medicine, 351, 13-22.

Chartrand, M. & Siegel, G. (2007). At war in Iraq and Afghanistan, Children in US military family. Ambulatory Pediatrics, 7, 1-2.

Cherry, N., Creed, F., Silman, A., etal. (2001). Health and exposures to United Kingdom Gulf War Veterans. Part-I: The pattern and extent of ill health. Occupational & Environmental Medicine, 58, 2291-2298.

Compas, B. E., Connonr-Smith, J. K., Saltzman, J. K. , Thompsen, A. H., & Wadsworth, M. E. (2000). Coping with stress during childhood and adolescence: Problem, progress and potential in theory and research. *Psychological Bulletin, 127,* 87-127.

Cozolino, L(2002). *The Neuroscience of Psychotherapy.* W.W. Norton and co.

Cozza, S., Chun, R. & Pollo, J. (2005). Military families and children during operation Iraqi freedom. *Psychiatric Quarterly, 76(4),* 371-378.

Cutler, M. (2011). Do we still arm force when we don't secure our own borders? CAPS senior Fellow; and senior special agent. INS (Ret.).

Davis, R. T. (2010). *U.S. Foreign Policy and National Security: Chronology and Index for the 20th Century.* Praeger Security International Series, Retrieved 25 September 2010.

Dawson, D. A. (2003). *Methodological issues in measuring alcohol use. Alcohol Res Health, 27(1),*18-29.

De Jong, K., der Kam, S., Ford, N. Hargreaves, S., van Oosten, R., Cunningham, D., Boots, G., Andrault, E. & Kleiber, R. (2007). The trauma of ongoing conflict and displacement in Chechnya : Quantitative assessment of living conditions and psychosocial and general health status among war displaced in Chechnya and Ingushetia. *Conflict & Health, 1(4),* 1-13.

Dekel, R., Solomon, Z. & Bleich, A. (2005). Emotional distress and marital adjustment of caregivers: contribution of level of impairment and appraised burden. *Anxiety, Stress and Coping, 18(1), 71-82.*

Deol, I. S. (1963). *Discussions for S. S. B. Interviews and college students.* Chandigarh: Minerva Academy.

Dirkzwager, A., Bramensen, I., Adler, H., & van der Ploeg, H. (2005). Secondary traumatization in partners, and parents of Dutch peacekeeping soldiers. Journal of Family Psychology, 19(2), 217-226.

Doyle, M & Peterson, K.(2005). Re-entry and re-integration: Returning home after combat. Psychiatric Quarterly, 76(4), 361-370.

Drummet A.R., Coleman M. & Cable S. (2003). Military Families under stress: Implications for family life education. Family Relations, 52(3), 279-287.

Drummet, A. R., Coleman, M., & Cable, S. (2003). Military families under stress: Implication for family life education. Family Relations, 52, 279-287.

Durand Bush, N. and Salmela, J.H. (2001). The Ottawa Mental Skills Assessment Tool (OMSAT-3). The Sport Psychologist. 15, 1-19.

Elder, G. H., Jr., & Clipp, E. C. (1989). Combat experience and emotional health: Impairment and resilience in later life. Journal of Personality, 57. 311-341.

Eric ,M., Flake, B.E. D., Patti, L. J., Laura S. (2009). The psychosocial effects of deployment on military children. Dev. Pediatrics, 30 (4).

Feeney, B. & Collins, N. (2004). Interpersonal safe heavens and secure base caregiving processes in adulthood. In S. Rholes, & J. Simsons Eds., Adult attachment: Theory, research and clinical implications (pp. 330-338). New York: Guilford.

Fiedler, N., Ozakinci, G., Hallman, W., Wartenberg, D., Brewer, N. T., , Barrett, D. H., & Kiepen, H. M. (2006). Military deployment to the gulf war as a risk factor for psychiatric illness among us troop. The British Journal of Psychiatry, 188, 453-459.

Figley, C. (1983). Catastrophe: An overview of family reactions. In C. Figley and H McCubbin (Eds)., Stress and the Family (pp. 3-20). New York: Brunner.

Fisher, and Crandle (1997). Complex attachment: Pattern of relating in the couples. Sexual and Marital Therapy, 12(3), 211-233.

Fonagy, P. (2001). *Attachment theory and psychoanalysis.* New York: Other Press.

Fontana, A., & Rosenheck , R. (1998). Psychological benefit and liabilities of traumatic exposures in the war zone. *Journal of Traumatic stress, 11,* 485-503.

Friedman, M. J. (2011). *1 in 8 returning soldier suffer from PTSD.* msnbc.com.

Fukunda, K., Nisenbaum, R., Stewart, g. et al, (1998). *Chronic multi symptom illness affecting air force veterans of the Gulf War. JAMA, 280,* 981-988.

George, C., & Solomon, J. (1999). Loss and bereavement: Attachment theory and recent controversies concerning "grief work" and the nature of detachment. In J. Cassidy, & P. Shavers (Eds.), *Handbook of attachment. Theory, research and clinical applications (pp. 735-759).* New York: Guilford.

Gittings, J. (1969). *The role of the Chinese Army.* New Delhi: Army Publisher.

Goldenson, R.M. (Ed). (1984). *Longman dictionary of Psychology and Psychiatry.* New York: Longman

Grant, B. F., Stinson, F. S., & Harfort, T. C. (2001). Age at onset of alcohol use and DSM-IV, alcohol abuse and dependence: A 12 year follow up. *Journal of Substance Abuse, 13,* 493-504.

Haftendorn, H. (1991). "The Security Puzzle: Theory-building and discipline-building in international security". *International Studies Quarterly ,* 35 (1): 3–17.

Hall, D. P & Jansen, J. A. (1995). Stress and arousal in deployment of a combat support Hospital. *Military Medicine, 160 (11),* 58-583.

Hallman, W. K., Kipen, H. M., & Diefenback, M. et. Al. (2003). *Symptoms pattern among Gulf war registry Veteran, American Journal of Public Health, 93,* 624-630.

Hammermeister, J., Michael A. P. & Carl J. O. (2009). Teaching Mental skills for self-esteem enhancement in a military healthcare settings . *Journal of Instructional Psychology,*

Hartta, Y., Zinta, R. L., & Tiwari, A. K. (2009). Appraisal of HIV-AIDS consciousness among college youths in Himachal Pradesh. Social Change, 39 (3), 406-428.

Hazan, C., Gur-Yaish, N., & Campa, M. (2004). What does it means to be attached? In S. Rholes, & J. Simson's (Eds), Adult attachment; Theory, research and clinical implications .(pp. 55-85). New York: Guilford.

Helm, M., Kulla, M, Birkenmaier, H, Hauke, J. & Lampl, L. (2007). Improved data quality by pen computer assisted emergency room data re cording following major trauma in the military setting. European Journal of Trauma and Emergency Surgery, 1, 52-58.

Hendrix, C., Jurich, A., Schumm, W. (1995). Long-term impact of Vietnam war service on family environment and satisfaction. Families in societies: The Journal of Contemporary Human Services, 76(8), 498-506.

Herbert, I. (2007). British soldier go awol because army ignores mental health problems. independent.co.uk.

Herrman, H., Saxena, S., & Moodie, R. (2005).Promoting mental health: Concept, emerging evidence and practice. A report of the World Health Organization, Department of Mental Health ad Substance Abuse, in collaboration with the University of Melbourne. Geneva: WHO.

Herzog, J. & Everson, R. (2010). *Secondary traumatic stress, deployment phase, and military families:* Systematic approaches to treatment. In B Everson & C. Figley (Eds.), *Families under fire: Systematic therapies with military families.* Routledge : Psychological Stress Series.

Herzog, J. R., Everson, R. B., & Whitworth, J. B. (2011). Do secondary trauma symptoms in spouse of combat –explodes national guard soldiers mediate impact of social trauma exposure on their children. *Child Adolescent Social Work Journal.* Published by Springer Science.

Hesse, E. (1999). The adult attachment interview: Historical and current perspective. In J. Cassidy & P. Shaver (Eds.), Handbook of attachment, theory, research and clinical applications (pp. 394-433). New York: Guilford.

Hiew, C. C. (1992). Separated by their network:Families with father living apart. Environment & Behaviour, 24, 206-225.

Hoge, C. W., Terhakopian, A., Castro, C. A., Messer, S. C. & Engel, C. C. (2007). Association of post-traumatic stress disorder with somatic symptoms, health care visit and absenteeism among Iraq War Veterans. American Journal of Psychiatry, 164(1), 150-*153.*

Hoge, C., Castro, C., Messer, S., McGurk, D., Cotting, D. & Koffman, R. (2005). Combat duty in Iraq and Afghanistan, mental health problems, and barrier to care. The New England Journal of Medicine, 362(2), 101-109.

Hoge, C., Castro, C., Messer, S., McGurk, D., Cotting, D., & Koffman, R. (2005). Combat duty in Iraq and Afghanistan, mental health problems, and barrier to care. The New England Journal of Medicine, 351(1), 13-22.

Hugh, S & de Girolambo, S. (2007). The experience of Military sexual trauma and rehabilitation for individual with spinal cord injury/dysfunction. Sexual Disabilities, 25, 65-72.

ICF International. (n.d.). Demographics 2007 profile of the Military Community. Washington, D.C. Military Community and family policy. Retrieved August 2009 from http:// cs.mhf.dod.mil/content/dav/mhf/qol.

Ikin, J.F., Sim, M.R., McKenzie, D.P., Horsley, K.W.A., Wilson, E.J., Harrex, W.K., et al. (2009). Life satisfaction and quality in Korean War veterans five decades after the war. Journal of Epidemiology & Community Health, 63, 359-365.

International Peace Bureau, Geneva (2002). The Military's impact on environment. Geneva.

IOWA Persian Gulf Study Group (1997). *Self reported illness and health status among Gulf War Veteran –a population based study. JAMMA, 277,* 238-245.

James, M. (2006). Developmental social policy: Theory and practice *Casa Asian Journal of Social Policy, 2(1),* 1-22.

James, S. (2010). Human security: Key drivers, antecedents and conceptualization. *Working Paper No. 1.* USA: Latrobe University.

Jiegen, Z. (2007). Contemporary Indian strategic culture & its nuclear strategy. *International Review Spring, 46.*

John, T. C., Harry, T. R. & Alex, J. Z. (2011). The value of social fitness with an application to the military. *American Psychological Association, 66* (1), 43–51.

Jose A. S., Donald, S. S. & Mark, E. B. (2007). *Burden of Disease and Costs of Illness.* Scientific Working Group, Report on Dengue, 1-5 October 2006.Geneva: World Health Organization .

Kahn, R.L., Wolfe, D.M., Quinn, R.P. & Snock, J.D. (1964). *Organizational Stress: Studies in role conflict and ambiguity.* New York: Wiley.

Kang, H.K., Bullman, T.A., & Taylor, J.W. (2006). Risk of selected cardiovascular diseases and posttraumatic stress disorder among former World War II prisoners of war. *Annals of Epidemiology, 16,* 381-386.

Kashes, R. J. (1996). The care of those returned: Psychiatric illnesses of war. In Ursano, Robert J. & Norwood, Ann E. (Eds.), *emotional aftermath of the Persian Gulf War: veterans, families, communities and nations.* Washington, DC : American Psychiatric Press.

Kelly, M.L., Herzog Simmer, P.A. & Harris, M.A. (1994). Effects of Military inducted separation on the parenting stress and family functioning of deploying mothers. *Military Psychology, 6(2),* 125-138.

Kelly, M.L., Holk E., Bonney J.F., Jervis M.S., Smith K.M. and Gaffney M.A. (2001). Navy Mothers experiencing and not *experiencing deployment: Reasons for staying in or learning the military. Military Psychology, 13(1),* 55-71.

Kulka, R.A., Schlenger, W.E., Fairbook, J.A., Hough, R.L., Jordon, B.K., Marmar, C.R., et al. (1990). *Trauma and the Vietnam veterans readjustment study.* New York: Brunner/Mazel, Inc.

La Grone, D. A. (1978). The military family syndrome. *American Journal of Psychiatry, 135,* 1040-1043.

Larner, B., Blow, A. (2011) : A model of meaning making coping and growth in combat veterans. *Review of General Psychology, 15(3), Sep* 2011, 187-197

Lazarus, R. S. & Folkman, S. (1984). *Stress, appraisal and coping.* New York: Springer.

Leopold, J. (2011). *Mental health and religion in the US Military: "Army's Spiritual Fitness Test"* comes under *fire.* Global Research, E-Newsletter 5 January, 2011

Lerner, Y. & Zilber, N. (1996). Psychological distress among recent immigrants from the soviet union to Israel. *Psychological Medicine, 26(3),*

Lester, D. (1995). War and suicide in France, 1850-1913. *Psychological Reports, 77(1),* 130-135.

Levinger, G. (1983). Development and change. In H.H. Kelley, et al. (Eds.), *Close relationships. (pp. 315–359).* New York: W.H. Freeman and Company.

Linely, P. A., & Joeph, S. ((2004). Positive change following trauma and adversity: *A review. Journal of Trauma Stress, 17,* 1-21.

Linn, S., Linn, R., Segal, D. R., Sheps, S., Levi, L., & Revach, M. (2011). Life satisfaction among Israeli soldiers with penetrating head wounds. *Armed Forces & Society,* 1-31.

Majumdar, B. N. (1963*). A study of Indian military History.*

Manjul, M. & Zinta, R. L. (2010). Depression as a devil in the human development: A case study. *Journal of Community Guidance & Research, 27 (1),* 103-112.

Manjul, M., & Zinta, R. L. (2008). Motivational approaches as a predictor of strategies for utilizing forest resources to economic development. Nava Arthiki, 16, 2A, 1-23.

Mansor, A.T. (2009). A preliminary study on occupational stress and job satisfaction among male Navy personnel at Naval Base in Lumut, Malaysia Nor Liyana , MOHD BOKTI, The Journal of International Social Research, 2 (9).

Marchant, K., & Medway, E. (1987). Adjustment and achievement associated with mobility in military families. Psychology in School, 24, 289-294.

Mark J. B. & Bowlest, S. V. (2011). Review of well-being in the context of suicide prevention and resilience. Maryland: Defense Centers of Excellence for Psychological Health & Traumatic Brain Injury (DCoE).

Marvin, R., Cooper, G., Hoffman, K., & Powell, B. (2002). The circle of security project: Attachment based intrventionwith care-giver pre-schools child's dyads. Attachment & Human Development, 4, 107-124.

McCubbin, H. I., , Joy, C. B., Cauble, A. B., Comeau, J. K. , Paterson, J. M., & Needle, R. H. (1980). Family stress and coping: A decade review. Journal of Marriage & family, 42, 855-871.

McCubin, H. I. & Patterson, J. (1982). Family strains. In H. McCubbin & A. Thompson (Eds), Family assessment for research and practices. Madison: University of Wisconsin.

Mental Health Advisory Team V. (2008). Operation Iraqi Freedom 06-08. Washington, DC: Office of the Surgeon: Multinational Force Iraq and Office of the Surgeon General, US Army Medical Command. from http://www.armymedicine.army.mil/reports/mhat/mhat_v/Redacted1-MHATV-OIF-4-FEB-2008Report.pdf

Milliken, C. S., Auchterlonie, J. L., & Hoge, C. W. (2007). Longitudinal assessment of mental health problems among active and reserve component soldiers returning from the Iraq war. *Journal of the American Medical Association, 298,* 2141-2148.

Mmari, K. N., Bradshaw, C. P., & Sudhinaraset, M. (2010). Exploring the role of social connectedness among youths. Perception from youth's parents and school personnel. *Child Youth Care Forum, 39,* 351-366.

Murithi, T. (2006). African Approaches to Building. Peace and Social Solidarity. *African Journal on Conflict Resolution, 6* (2),

Nathan, F. (2011). Water related natural risks as insecurity. *Fifth Pan-European International Relations Conference.* Netherland: The Hague.

National Association of Adult Protective Services Administration Position Paper on self –neglect. *National Committees for prevention of adult abuse.*

Newby, J. H., McCarroll, J. E., Ursano, R. J., Fan, Z. Z., Shigimura, J., & Tucker-Harris, Y. (2005). Positive and negative consequences of military deployment. *Military Med, 170,* 815-819.

Nigel D. W. & Sorcha, M. (2008). EU Operations and private military contractors: Issues of corporate and institutional responsibility. *EJIL, 19(5),* 965-988.

Orthner, D. (2002). Deployment and separation adjustment among Army civilian spouses. *Survey Report.* Retrieved June 30, 2004, from *http://www.armymwr.com/corporate/operations/plannings/survey.asp.*

Orthner, D.K., Bower, G.L. & Beare, V.G. (1990). The organization family: A question of work and family boundaries, marriage and family review, *15,* 15-36.

Owens G.P, Stegar M.F, Whitesell A. A., & Herrera C.J. (2009). Post-traumatic stress disorder, guilt, depression, meaning in life among military veterans. *Journal of Instructional Psychology,* 654-657

Ozesmi, Y. (2006). Fuzzy cognitive maps of local people by dam construction, their demands regarding resettlement. Department of environment engineering. Ozesmi. Org.

Pajares (2002). Overview of social cognitive theory and of self-efficacy. Retrieved February, 30, 2009, from http://www.emory.edu/EDUCATION/mfp//eff.html.

Paleri, P. (2008). *National Security: Imperatives and challenges.* New Delhi: Tata McGraw-Hill.

Pantelogiannis, F. (2003). Russian military reform. A Master Thesis. Institut Europeen des hautes etudes internationals.

Parkkari, A. et al. (2011). Neuromuscular training with injury prevention counseling to decrease the risk of acute musculoskeletal injury in young men during military service: a population-based, randomized study. BMC Medicine, 9, 35

Patrick, B. (2000). Psychological Aspects of Recruitment: conception for the Swiss Army XXI. Department of Applied Psychology, University of Zurich.

Port, C.L., Engdahl, B., Frazier P. & Eberly, R. (2002). Factors related to the long-term course of PTSD in older ex-prisoners of war. *Journal of Clinical Geropsychology, 8,* 203-214.

Port, C.L., Engdahl, B., Frazier, P., & Eberly, R. (2002). Factors related to the long-term course of PTSD in older ex-prisoners of war. *Journal of Clinical Gyro psychology, 8,* 203-214.

Purushothaman, U. (2010). Shifting perceptions of power: soft power and India's foreign policy. Journal of piece studies, 17, 2&3, A.

Raddatz, M. (2010). Soldiers take medications for stress. Abc NEWS.com.

Rescul, C., Joseph, S., & Erdal, T. (2011). The Psychological cost of war: Military combat and mental health. *http://aysps.gsu.edu/uwrg-research.html/*

Rice, V.J., Butler, J., & Marra, D.(1996). *Predicting performance: self-esteem among soldiers attending health care specialist training.* Texas; Army research laboratory.

Robert M. B. Mary E. M. (1992). Progress toward eliminating Drug and Alcohol Abuse among vs. Military personnel. *Armed Forces & Society, 18 (4)*, 476-496.

Rutter, M. (1993). Resilience: Some conceptual considerations. *Journal of Adolescent Health Care, 14*, 626-631.

Ryan, R.M., & Deci, E. L. (2001). On happiness and human potentials: A review of research on hedonic and eudaimonic well-being. *Annual Review of Psychology, 52*, 141-166.

Sartorius. N (1990). Preface. In D.Goldberg and D. Tantam (eds), *The public health impact of mental disorders.* Toronto: Hogrefe and Huber.

Schnurr, P.P., Spiro, A., Aldwin, C.M., & Stukel, T.A. (1998). Physical symptom trajectories following trauma exposure: Longitudinal findings from the normative Aging Study. *Journal of Nervous & Mental Disease, 186*, 522-528.

Schok, M. L. , Kleber, R. J., Elands, M., & Weerts, J. M. (2008). *Meaning as mission: A review of empirical studies on appraisal of war and peacekeeping experience. Clinical Psychology Review, 28*, 357-365.

Schuckit, M. A., Smith, T. L. & Chacko, Y. (2006). Evaluation of a depression related model of alcohol problems in 430 propends from the San Diego prospective study. *Drug Alcohol Dependence, 82(3)*, 194-203.

Seal, K. H., Bertenthal, D., Miner, C. R., Sen, S., & Marmar, C. (2007). *Bringing the war back home: Mental health disorder among 103788 US Veteran returning from Iraq Afghanistan seen at department of Veteran Affairs facilities. Arch. International Med. 167*, 476-482.

Shahrbanou, T. (2010). Human security: Concepts and implication with an application to post-intervention challenges in Afghanistan. *European Journal of Scientific Research, 44(4)*, 660-665.

Sharma, A., & Zinta, R. L. (2008). Alcoholism: A case study. *Indian Journal of Psychology & Mental Health, 1(2)*, 195-214.

Singh, S. H. & Zinta, R. L. (2008). DHAT Syndrome: A case study. Journal of Community Guidance & Research, 25 (2), 173-184.

Smith, D. & Stohl, R. (2000). The evolving role of military forces in human security. USA: Centre for defense information.

Smith, S. & Haythom, W. S. (1972). Effect of compatibility, crowding, group size, and leadership seniority on stress, axiety, hostility and annoyance in isolated groups. Journal of Personality & Social Psychology, 22(1), 67-79.

Solomon, Z., Waysman, M., Levy, G., Fried, B., Mikulincer, M., & Benbenishty, R., (1992). From front line to home front: A study of secondary traumatization. Family Process, 31, 289-302.

Spector, P.E. (1985). Measurement of human service staff satisfaction: Development of the job satisfaction. Survey. American Journal of Community Psychology, 13, 693-713.

Spiro, A., Schnurr, P.P., & Aldwin, C.M. (1994). Combat-related *posttraumatic stress disorder symptoms in older men. Psychology& Aging, 9,* 17-26.

Spiro, A., Schnurr, P.P., & Aldwin, C.M. (1997). A life-span perspective on the effects of military service. Journal of Geriatric Psychiatry, 30, 91-128.

Subramaniam, T. S. (2009). Of men and mind. Frontline, 26(23),

Sudin, J., Fear, N. T., Hull, S. Jones, N., Dandekar, C., Hotof, M., Wessely, S.,& Rona, R.. J. (2010). Rewarding and un-rewarding aspect of deployment to Iraq and its association with psychological stress in U. K. military personnel. International. Arc. Occupational Environmental health, 83, 653-663.

Tanielian, T., Jaycox, L., Schell, T., Marshall, G., Burnam, M., Eibner, C. (2008). *Invisible wound of war: Summary and recommendation for addressing psychological and cognitive injuries.* Santa Monica: Rand Corporation.

Tanielin, T. & Jaycox, L., Eds. (2008). Invisible wounds of war: Psychological and cognitive injuries, their consequences, and services

to assist recovery. Santa Monica, California: RAND. http://www.rand.org/pubs/monographs/2008/RAND_MG720.pdf

Terri, T., & Lisa, H. J. (Ed) (2008). *Invisible would of war:* Psychological and cognitive injuries their consequences and service and service to assist recoveries. *www.RAND.org.*

Tidball, K. G. & Marianne, E. K. (2010). Greening in the red zone. In K. G. Tidball and E. K. Marianne (Eds.), *Nature of engagement to fFoster resilience in military communities.* Verlag: Springer.

Todd B. K., Terri, J., Keith, M., & Gitendra, U. (2006). Social anxiety and posttraumatic stress in combat veterans: Relations to well-being and character strengths. *Behaviour Research & Therapy, 44,* 561–583.

van Dyk, G. ( ). The role of military psychology in peacekeeping operations: the South African national defense force as an example

Verma, Amita, Mahajan , A & Verma S.K. (1989). A co-relationship study of two well-being scales. *Journal Personality and Clinical Studies, 5, (1)* 93-95.

Wang, S. J., Salihu, M., Rushiti, F., Bala, L, & Modwig, J. (2010). Survivors of the war in the Northern Kosovo: Violence exposure, risk factors and public health effects of an ethnic conflict. *Conflict & Health, 4(11),* 1-16.

Whitlock, J. (2006). Youth perception of life at school: Contextual correlates of school connectedness in adolescence. *Applied Developmental Science, 10,* 13-29.

William B. B. (2008). Another Emerging "Storm": Iraq and Afghanistan Veterans with PTSD. *The Criminal Justice System,* 5 (2),

Wolf, J. Brown, P. J., & Kelley, J. M. (1993). Re-assessing war stress: Exposure and Persian Gulf-war. *Journal of Social Issues, 49,* 15-31.

Yu, Su. (1954). Deputy Chief Staff. *JMJP,* 31 July, 1954.

Zeiss, R.A., & Dickman, H.R. (1989). PTSD 40 years later: Incidence and person-situation correlates in former POWs. *Journal of Clinical Psychology, 45,* 80-87.

Zimmerman, P. d. (2011). Science since 9/11: Homeland insecurity. *Nature, 477,* 153-154.

Zinta, R. L. & Tiwari, A. K. (2006). Impact of socio-economic status on performance among male and female secondary students of Himachal Hill State. *Nava Arthiki, 14,* 2, 1-7.

Zinta, R. L. & Tiwari, A. K. (2006). Relationship between self-efficacy, socio-economic status and performance in secondary students. *Research Journal Social Sciences, 14, (1),* 121-137.

Zinta, R. L. (2006). Effect of self-efficacy, test-anxiety and short-term intervention on problem solving: A preliminary analysis. *Social Science International, 22*(1), 3-8.

Zinta, R. L. (2006). Is guided mastery helpful in problem solving. *Psychological Studies, 51(4),* 323-325.

Zinta, R. L. (2008). Effectiveness of guided mastery treatment for reducing test-anxiety among self-efficacious students. *Journal of Indian Academy of Applied Psychology, 34(2),* 233-239.

Zinta, R. L. (2008). Socio-economic status as a panacea for mental health: A note on displaced families of Bhakra Dam. *Nava Arthiki, 16, 2A, 49-74.*

Zinta, R. L. (2009). Bharat mein uch shiksha ki dasha aur disha. *Sanchar Bulletin, 1(1),* 104-106.

Zinta, R. L. (2009). Different facets of quality of life among the populace of mounting India in 21st century. *Akhil Bhartiya Shodh Seminar on Iksavin sadi mein Bharat: Dasha avam disha,* organized by University Grant Commission, New Delhi. Dayanand Vedic Snatkotar Mahavidyalaya, Urai, Jalon, U. P.

Zinta, R. L. (2009). Different facets of quality of life among the populace of mounting Indian in 21st century. A paper presented in National seminar on Ikswi Sadi mein Bharat ki disha avam Dasha. Urai: Jalon.

Zinta, R. L. (2010). Dimensions of quality of life in the tribal areas of Kinnaur: A caste-wise analysis. A Research Project proposal approved by Institute of Tribal Research and Studies, H. P. University, Summer Hill, Shimla-171005.

Zinta, R. L. (2010). Performance among high and low self-efficacious students. In P, Ramalingam (Ed.), *Recent studies in school psychology*. Delhi: Authors Press.

Zinta, R. L. (2010). *Psychology Manual*. New Delhi: H. G. Publications.

Zinta, R. L. (2010). *Reservation and inclusive growth*. A paper presented in Conference organized by Public Administration Department, HPU.

Zinta, R. L. (2011). Need of cognitive-behavioural model for sustainable development. A research paper presented at National seminar, Economic Department HPU.

Zinta, R. L., & Tiwari, A. K. (2007). Impact of guided mastery treatment on self-efficacy among test-anxious students. *Journal of Psychological Researches, 51*(2), 91-101.

Zinta, R. L., & Tiwari, A. K. (2008). Socio-economic and infrastructure facilities for sustainable rural development: A factorial analysis on Himachal Pradesh. A project Reported submitted to the *Integrated Institute of Himalayan Studies*, HPU Shimla-171005.

Zinta, R. L., Negi, S. R. & Thakur, R. (2010). Caste and efficacy as a precursor of cognitive abilities: A study on tribal high school students of District Kinnaur. *Research Journal Social Science, 18(1)*, 130-157.

Zoroya, G. (2011). Strain on forces in the field at a five-year high. *USA Today, 85*, 7.

INDEX

A

B

C

D

E

F

G

I

❍❍❍